A Beginning Actor's Companion

Fourth Edition

Lani Harris
Susan Hargrave Pate
Randy Wonzong
Donna Breed
California State University

KENDALL/HUNT PUBLISHING COMPANY
4050 Westmark Drive   Dubuque, Iowa 52002

Copyright © 1989, 1992, 1996, 2008 by Kendall/Hunt Publishing Company

ISBN 978-0-7575-5171-0

Printed in the United States of America
10 9 8 7 6 5 4 3 2

Contents

Acknowledgments

Special thanks to Tom Langkau, for his endless support and patience; to Sarah Pressler, Marketing and Public Relations Manager at The Round House Theatre, Washington, D.C., for coming through in the eleventh hour.

Our thanks to those who worked on previous editions of this text—Gayle Elliot, Mercedes Frontera-Gilbert, Gail Holbrook, Virginia Storie-Crawford, Ted Wendt, Richard Wilson, Lynn Marler Cynthia Lammel, and William Johnson—for their insights, field-testing, and proofreading of this material.

And to our Beginning Acting students, whose responses to these techniques always teach us more than we teach them.

Lani Harris, Susan Hargrave Pate, Randy Wonzong, and Donna Breed

Getting Started

WHAT IS ACTING?

The origin of acting begins with ritual and storytelling. According to theatre historians and cultural anthropologists, acting is as old as the first humans sitting around the prehistoric campfire playing out the roles of demons, hunted animals, or even rain spirits for the gathered community. Moreover, acting is also one of the easiest and most natural things that each of you do every day. In fact, people become expert performers of many roles in daily life, without taking any acting courses all.

Examine any situation in your own life where you have accomplished something, or attained a goal, small or large. You focused your energies and attention on a specific set of circumstances. You knew what you wanted to achieve, you were aware of what was standing in your way, and you performed one or more actions to obtain your goal. In its most fundamental form, that is what acting is, and that is the basis of this text.

Basically, acting is a very natural thing to do. We simply don't always consider our behavior to be acting, yet there are many times each day, perhaps hundreds of times, when you are acting. You choose specific behaviors and actions in order to achieve a goal.

The important difference is the degree to which you control and alter your behavior, modify your actions, and adjust your choices. If you consciously select a specific goal or outcome, and if you willfully modify your behavior to achieve that goal, then you are acting. Acting is often assumed to be a creative form of pretending or "lying." Actually, nothing could be further from the truth. A good actor works very hard to live truthfully within the character; to react honestly, as the character would, within the specific circumstances in which the character exists. An actor puts themselves into the same situation.

Let's say the situation is that of Shakespeare's *Romeo and Juliet*, and the actor is playing Romeo. He must first analyze all of the factors that affect Romeo. The actor would have to evaluate what Romeo faces:

a. He falls deeply, madly in love with Juliet, and marrying her becomes his life goal.
b. His family hates her family, and visa versa.
c. The whole town is aware of the feud, so he must be very careful in whom he confides.
d. Juliet is closely watched by her family, so it is difficult to find time with her.
e. Given the family feud, neither family will agree to a marriage.

As an actor playing Romeo, you would have to personalize the depth of Romeo's feelings, his urgency, and his passion in order to take the actions that Romeo takes in the play, as if it were you. You would have to find the truthfulness in Romeo's feelings that cause him to take the actions that he does. As an actor, you control your own thoughts and behavior, using yourself, your body, your voice, and your understanding of Romeo, to act the part honestly, as though it were happening to you.

Frankly, if you were not a good actor you would never have survived the second grade, let alone become a young adult. It is a set of skills we all have and use all the time. You have goals and needs every day. Some of them are as simple as getting to class on time; some are as passionate and urgent as Romeo trying to marry his true love. In each of your own life situations, you "take action" in the form of behavior, to try to get what you need. You make choices about what actions you must take to overcome obstacles that stand in your way. Sometimes these behaviors or "actions" are well thought out, sometimes they are ruled by your emotions. Sometimes your actions are successful, sometimes they are a spectacular mistake with negative consequences. It is exactly the same for every character you encounter as an actor.

This book focuses on how to use those skills you already possess in actual drama performances of scenes from real plays. We will begin by doing simple activities very much like real life situations, and then our focus will shift to scripted dialogue written by playwrights, because the larger aim of this course is to enable you to perform characters created by people like Tennessee Williams, Beth Henley, or William Shakespeare.

Acting on stage, however, is a more complex process than "acting" in social situations. It is a more specific, more conscious process. Acting can be defined as a character *in a situation* who *willingly takes action* to overcome *a known difficulty* which prevents the achievement of *a desired goal*. That is a pretty dense and concise definition, and in the process of working through this semester we will explore the details and techniques of that statement of acting. For now let us briefly define each of the important pieces in the statement:

"in a situation" is the actual, **given circumstances** of the scene; for example, in the roommate situation, the given circumstance would be a typical two-person dorm room early on a school day morning,

"willingly takes action" is the thing (or things) the character *chooses* to do, and the action they take; in other words, **the tactics** a character uses to achieve some desired goal,

"a known difficulty" is what stands in the character's way, **the obstacle** which keeps the character from achieving some desired goal,

"a desired goal" is the thing the character wants, the goal, **the intention** that makes the character commit the actions of the play. This desired goal must be very important to the character; this importance is referred to as **the stakes.** In other words, what will happen to this character if they do not achieve their goal?

Now, if we substitute these terms in the statement about what acting is, we can conclude that: **Acting can be defined as a character in given circumstances that uses tactics to overcome obstacles which prevent the achievement of an important intention.**

WHAT IS A PLAY?

Our definition of acting so far talks about you as the character, but most plays are written with more than one character. In fact, plays usually present us with one or two central characters and show us their interactions with a number of other characters in the course of the play. It is exactly this interaction that is most central to acting and which draws most of us to theatre and to acting in general.

It is true that acting is all about a character doing something to overcome an obstacle to achieve a goal. But the play itself, the drama, is about the clash between different characters with opposing goals or intentions; the "drama" in a play is the result of what happens when differing characters meet and interact. In its most concise definition, **drama is conflict.**

In its simplest form a play presents us with one character who wants something which another character in the play either has or also wants. As the play goes on, each character tries to achieve his or her goal in spite of the obstacle the other character is or represents. The clash between the two characters is what we call **conflict**; it is the result of opposing intentions meeting head-on. It is what happens when two highly motivated characters, each with a strong but opposite intention, meet and attempt to achieve their separate goals. And this is often the most interesting part of any play. It is where the major energy, the tension of the play lies; and to be quite honest, these moments of clash and intense interaction are the parts actors most like to play—the big moments where the opposing forces clash in some fine dramatic struggle.

Let's create an example closer to real life: Imagine you are in class and you have not done the reading assignment, and the instructor begins the discussion, to make certain that the students understand the material. Each of you has a clear intention. As the teacher calls on you, he or she is merely trying to achieve an intention, to see if you are keeping up. However, by calling on you—incidentally, this action is a **tactic** the teacher uses to achieve an **intention**—it presents you with a big **obstacle:** how are you going to succeed at appearing to be prepared if you have not read the material? That is the moment of character interaction, the essence of drama and acting. If we acted this scene out, the most interesting part would probably be that tense moment between when the instructor asked you the question and you tried to come up with an answer. What **tactic** will you choose? Will it help or hurt you?

Of course, plays are usually much longer and more complex than this example, but in their essence dramas are all alike on this point: they are about the process of clashing intentions, embodied by actors playing the roles of characters with opposing goals.

WHAT IS THE COLLABORATIVE PROCESS?

Throughout this text you are going to be working on exercises, activities, and, later, scripted scenes—all of which will require you to collaborate with other actors. It is important that you understand this process and realize some of its challenges and pitfalls.

For example, it should be clear to you by this point that if dramatic conflict arises out of characters clashing with each other, and if the best scenes are those with the strongest and clearest dramatic life, then the means of getting to a polished, well-rehearsed performance of any such exciting scene must include working with others. This means collaboration. In fact, it requires a lot of hard and exciting work. Collaboration, of course, includes a certain amount of practical business which we shall cover in detail later, such as being on time and well prepared for rehearsals, being courteous and respectful of each other's efforts, and doing careful script preparation.

But collaboration can also be a liberating, cooperative means of discovering and developing the life of the characters, their conflicts, and the life of the scene as a whole. Indeed, it is only in working with the other actors in your scenes that you truly discover and bring the performance of the characters to life. And it is only in working together during the rehearsal process that you can learn important things about the character you are playing, the other characters in your scene, and the play as a whole.

Certainly all of us can quickly see the need for actors to work well together; indeed, most of acting is working together with someone else. But when you collaborate, what you end up with is often very different from any one individual's ideas; it is a combination of the best of everybody's ideas, modified by rehearsal, and then modified again in performance by what actually happens in front of an audience.

Good collaboration is essential for good acting. Good collaborators are willing to explore and try out different ways of playing a scene, a speech, a reaction. Collaborators attempt to look at all ideas and then select those that make the project go forward in the most interesting way. Who thought up those ideas or where they came from is irrelevant in collaboration. What's important is that the actors work together toward a common goal: a truthful and believable performance.

There are perhaps only two basic rules contained within the principle of collaboration:

1. Experiment, explore, attempt alternate ways together to do the scene.
2. Work for the good of the performance, not for your individual ego.

These principles of collaboration, of working together fruitfully, are very important in acting. When you get into your assigned exercises and scenes, you'll find that you'll have some good ideas, your scene partner will have some good ideas, and some of the best ideas will come from your thinking and working together. Often no one can remember where the best ideas came from. They're truly the property of the group, and they'll only emerge when all concerned work together unselfishly toward truthful performances.

WHY ACTING EXERCISES?

Beginning acting students are almost always in a hurry to get going; they want scenes and characters assigned to them so they can get to work and start acting. They didn't sign up for a course just to find that it is made up of people running around and doing silly things in small groups. "Just give me a play to do. This is supposed to be my big chance to be somebody on stage!"

But acting is more than merely practicing to say lines of dialogue out loud, and it is more than just reading in a book about how to do acting. It is true that you can learn about lots of things intellectually, by studying ideas and principles through thinking, talking, and writing about them. That's one good way to learn about acting, but it isn't the only way, and for most actors it probably isn't the best way. In order to be a competent actor, you have to understand the principles of acting experientially by *doing them*, not just by reading about them.

Think of acting as a skill, like hitting a baseball or riding a skateboard: there are a certain number of ideas, rules, and theories that apply; but no matter how much you read about skateboards, you are not going to be able to balance on one and fly down the street and over curbs without specific physical skills, and gaining those skills takes a lot of practice.

So it is with acting. One of the main ways that you'll come to understand the principles of acting and master the skills of acting is by doing acting exercises in class. For a while you'll do all sorts of exercises, aimed at a variety of skills. Some of the exercises may seem strange or silly or uncomfortable, but all of them are useful. They all contain at least one important idea or technique or experience that will be important in helping you grow as an actor. Student actors find that they really understand the principles of acting only by discovering them experientially, through acting exercises.

The most important things that you need to know about acting exercises are these:

1. The only way to do acting exercises wrong is not to do them whole-heartedly.

There is no "right way" to do these exercises. That's because acting exercises aren't like math problems, where the important thing is coming up with the right answer. In acting exercises what's important is the **process** or the experience of the exercise, not the result. If you do the exercises with enthusiasm and commitment, the principle or technique will become evident to all concerned, and you'll understand it experientially as well as intellectually. You will discover why this "silly" exercise is relevant, and you will develop new skills.

2. At first everybody else will feel just as silly and conspicuous as you do.

If everybody's doing weird stuff, which is mostly what acting exercises seem to be about, then nobody's really silly or conspicuous, as long as they're really doing the exercise with enthusiasm and concentration.

3. In doing acting exercises, the only people who are conspicuous are those who don't commit themselves to trying to do the exercise, but instead either participate only half-heartedly or not at all. There's no place for "cool," or for attitude in an acting class. Everyone must let go of individual ego, and open themselves up to making discoveries. Performing really only works—has an effect on the audience, sweeps them up, shows them some truths about life that they didn't know—when the performers commit to it totally.

STAGE FRIGHT

Stage fright is something that affects all of us; it is a natural, human response to being the center of attention in a group—such as being an actor on stage, of course. But it applies to a great many life situations where others are an audience for what you do: having to speak to a group, demonstrating a particular skill—such as a dance step, or even wearing a new swim suit in public the first day of the season.

Stage fright stems from the primal "Fight or Flight" response. It is a natural way for your body to react to perceived danger. Being in the spotlight like this causes your body stress. When faced with such stress, the body automatically begins to try to cope with this situation in physical ways. Most noticeably, your heart rate will increase; your breathing will become more rapid and shallow. You may feel a tingling, floating sensation in your stomach region. For some people the body reactions get more and more complex: sweating, a damp and clammy feeling, difficult or stuttered speech, dry mouth, nausea, dizziness, or a pressing need to go to the bathroom.

Beginning to feel a little nervous already? Well, the good news is that it is normal to feel some or most of the stage fright symptoms listed here. And for a lot of people, just thinking about being in front of an audience—as you are probably imagining yourself right now—triggers the same reactions as actually being up on the stage of a crowded theatre ready to perform. But there is more good news, too. Behavioral scientists have discovered that even the simple act of talking about **performance anxiety**— which is the term some of them use when they are talking about stage fright—helps reduce it for most people. Being able and willing to admit your own performance anxiety and being honest about having it actually makes you less nervous, and there are very specific techniques you can use to overcome this anxiety.

It is certainly common for most performers, novice or professional, to be nervous before a performance, and for beginning acting students, just standing in front of the group in a simple acting exercise is a nerve-wracking situation. But for most people, including most actors, efforts to deny or hide their anxiety only makes the symptoms worse. What you have to do is anticipate the symptoms, acknowledge them, adjust your behavior and make them help you, not hinder your performance.

Stage fright doesn't need to stop you from doing anything. You can deal with it so it doesn't cripple you. One of the main strategies in dealing with this anxiety is to learn about it: what it is, what you can do about it, and how you can keep it from paralyzing you.

We have already listed the typical reactions which your body will go through when you experience performance anxiety. They are common, normal responses to stress, and when you get them during the course of this class, realize they are not going to ruin your chances of success. They are a typical part of acting, but how you feel depends upon how you interpret and control these symptoms.

There are numerous useful things you can do to counteract the effects of stage fright.

1. **Prepare.** Be very well-prepared and well-rehearsed. Without a doubt the most important tool for handling your fears and anxieties about being a failure on stage is to be well practiced. If you've rehearsed enough, and rehearsed efficiently, you will feel confident; you are much less apt to lose lines or forget what you're doing, and therefore will be in much less danger of losing it onstage. The most common reason to "dry up" in performance, particularly auditions, is lack of rehearsal.

So rehearse, rehearse, rehearse, and then rehearse some more. Rehearse out loud, on your feet. Ask your friends to watch so you will have experience in front of people, and you will not panic in front of an audience. The better you know your material, the less chance you'll dry up onstage. Rehearsals help create a pattern (or habit) so that your mind and body know what comes next.

Without adequate preparation, none of the rest of these techniques will help you.

2. Focus. Fear is a distraction. It means that you have stopped focusing on your character's goal, and begun to think about your own fear . . . whether you are wondering if you can get the words right or if your fly is open, you have become "self"-conscious. You are no longer "in the moment" and it shows. You are likely to manifest this fear physically, by not making eye contact, developing nervous mannerisms or a defensive posture. Awareness of this distraction is the key to saving the moment.

As soon as you feel this fear, ask yourself "Who am I?", "What do I want?", and "How badly do I want it?". These questions are about the character you are playing, not yourself. This technique will bring you back into focus, on the character's intention/goal, and will at least provide you with enough information to ad lib, if you have lost a line.

When you have something to focus on, there will be a noticeable physical relaxation. When you are no longer thinking about the audience or your own fear, your body relaxes in a very natural way that can be read by an audience. You are back in control, and the audience goes back to watching the character's actions.

3. Breathe! This sounds silly and obvious, but when an actor becomes focused on fear, panic may develop. The aforementioned "Fight or Flight" response enabled primitive humans to either fight the enemy or run away. When your brain sends a "fear" message, your body responds immediately by flooding your bloodstream with a powerful chemical: adrenaline.

An excess of adrenaline causes all those physical symptoms listed earlier—dry mouth, shaking, sweating, bladder urgency, spasms, twitches, and much more. When this happens you are likely to tighten your chest and actually hold your breath, without being aware of it. Holding your breath will cause a lack of oxygen to your brain. A combination of less oxygen and an excess of adrenaline will have two immediate results: disorientation and paranoia—the last two things you need during a performance or audition!

Again, awareness of what is happening will save you. As soon as you feel any of these symptoms, breathe! Breathe deeply and slowly. You will regain control of your body by doing this. Hyperventilating will only make the problem worse. The oxygen that you breathe in will dilute the adrenaline in your bloodstream, and the physical symptoms will disappear. You will soon be back in the driver's seat.

4. Define your fear. In the days or hours before the performance, take some time to define exactly what you are afraid of. What is the worst that will happen? Be very specific.

Will you muff a line? *Then what?* Very likely, another actor will cover it. Or you will ad-lib. Or the stage manager may call out your line. If you know in advance what lines give you trouble, you can prepare a response. But if you mess up a line, something *will* happen next. What else makes you fearful? Will you faint? *Then what?* Someone will probably slap you or throw water in your face. . . . or they may have to drag your unconscious carcass offstage. What else? You may throw up? *Then what?* A very annoyed stagehand will have to clean it up. What else? You might wet your pants? *Then what?* The costumer will likely kill you!

Are you laughing yet? The key here is to name each fear, asking yourself *"Then what?"*. Carry this out until it is funny. One of the best ways to reduce the power of your fears is to laugh at them. And by defining exactly what you are afraid of, you can figure a way out. You can prepare a solution to each problem before it occurs.

5. Visualize Success. Take time before your performance or audition, preferably in a quiet, comfortable place where you can be alone without disturbance. Concentrate. Precisely imagine everything in your performance, in detail. Visualize it going beautifully. Visualize yourself doing very well. Go over that image in your mind until it is deeply ingrained.

Too often we make the mistake of visualizing what we are afraid of, and that negative image gets recorded in our subconscious. Instead, see yourself doing everything perfectly, overcoming every problem. Spend as much time with these positive images as you can. Refuse to let a negative image become established.

6. Use the energy. This technique can be a lifesaver, but some qualification is needed here: it will not work in every circumstance. It also does not mean that you allow the adrenalin to take over, creating a manic performance, words shooting out like a machine gun.

For whatever reason, there may come a time when you are not able to overcome your nerves, panic, or a personal emotion that has you in its grip. Say, for example, that moments before an audition or performance, the love of your life calls and breaks up with you, or you get word that someone you know has passed away. These are difficult emotions to fully control. What can you do? You can try to find a parallel between what is happening to your character and the emotion you are feeling. Channel all that energy into your character's goals or objective. This will heighten the stakes and give you a point of concentration, rather than letting your feelings become a distraction.

Once, when I was a struggling actress in Los Angeles, I was very late for the taping of a video project, due to circumstances beyond my control. Although the situation was explained to the director, who was graciously willing to wait for me, by the time I arrived, I was completely unnerved. Overwhelmed with worry about making a bad impression in a professional situation, I felt panic about the taping.

I had to find a way to focus. I looked for a parallel between what I was feeling and the part I was playing. The monologue I had been assigned for the taping was from *Anne of a Thousand Days*, the speech before Anne is taken to the gallows. At that moment, I could certainly relate to being killed in public. Coming up with that connection allowed me to take all of my personal anxiety and use it, in character, to fuel the speech. Knowing and utilizing this technique gave me a way to perform successfully and I received other jobs as a result of that performance. As I said, this doesn't work in every situation, but knowing how to do it can sometimes really turn things around.

Try to practice and repeat these six steps to become so familiar with them that they are automatic. As you practice and find that these steps really work, your confidence will increase, knowing that you *can* control the fear and that stage fright will not get in the way of your performance.

Concentration is a powerful tool against stage fright. Before you perform, take a few minutes to center your attention on what you're going to do, not on how you feel. Establish your breathing, do some neck rolls and a simple warm up. Remind yourself who your character is, where he is, and what he's trying to do or accomplish. Then go out onstage and do what you know needs to be done. If you've rehearsed well enough, and you concentrate on "doing," you won't have any extra brain—or heart—power to waste on worrying about stage fright.

CHAPTER ONE EXERCISES

Introductory Performance

The main requirement in acting is that you get up and do it. Thus, we start the class by having everyone get up and do something, just to break the ice. This is your introductory performance, and it is graded only as participation. If you do it, you will get full points. If you don't show up when you're scheduled, or don't do it at all, you will get an F.

You have a maximum of two minutes for your introductory performance during which you can do almost anything you like. You may work with a partner, if you wish, but only someone else from this class.

Here's what you can't do:

do not pantomime to a recording;
do not imitate an actor playing a role;
do not recite the lyrics from a song;
do not do something obscene or dangerous.

Here's what you can do: You can probably think of others:

sing a song;
play a musical instrument;
recite a poem;
read a very short story aloud;
play hackey-sack;
juggle;
do a short martial-arts demonstration;
tell a clean joke;
share your most embarrassing moment;
stand on your head;
do a magic trick;
do a cheer-leading routine;
paint your toenails while dressed as a pumpkin;
whistle two songs at once.

Remember, the only way to do this assignment wrong is not to do it. If you have an idea and aren't sure whether it will work, ask your teacher. Don't ask the teacher for help unless you have an idea in the first place. Figuring out what to do is part of the assignment. Don't be afraid to do something that makes you feel silly. That happens all the time in acting, and you must be willing to take that risk.

Contentless Scene

When you look at another actor's performances, you examine lots of things, beginning with the choices she has made about Intentions, Obstacles, and Tactics. You look at how that other actor physicalizes her character, and how well she listens and connects to other people on the stage. When it comes time for you to perform a scene, you do all the analysis you've already learned and put everything together in your performance.

Actors in plays are working on texts of plays—scripts—written by playwrights. They find the basis for their analyses in what the playwright has written. Most published playscripts are dense with possibilities and meanings; published scripts can be a little intimidating at first, until you have developed enough skill to find all of the possibilities.

For your first scene assignment in this class, you and your acting partner will be your own playwrights: you will create your own scene, analyze it, and perform it. You don't have to write a play. You'll use the words in the following Contentless Scenes. There are two versions for two actors and one version for three actors. Your teacher will assign you a partner (or partners), and you will work from one of the scripts which follow these instructions.

A contentless scene is one in which the words, by themselves, do not clearly reveal any specific characters or story; it is a scene that has no specified dramatic content. It is up to you and your scene partner to decide who the characters are, what their relationship is, and what happens in the scene.

You have the evidence (the words of the scene); your assignment is to figure out what is happening to the people in the scene that makes them say these words. It's like an iceberg: the words are only the tip, most of the interesting stuff is below the water line, or in the scene, unspoken. Think of the scene as a meaningful moment in these people's lives, a moment when some serious decisions have to be made. What happens between the lines—a pause to think, a decision to leave and then to stay—gives the scene its power, its believability, its realism.

The words from these scenes could have been said at a gravesite, a hospital bed, or a counselor's office. They could have been said between two friends who had a terrible argument and now want to patch things up. They could have been said because a wife is tired of her husband's alcoholism and is ready to leave for good. They could reflect the classical love triangle.

These are just a few ways the scenes could work. Now think of some possibilities for each of the scenes. Before you meet with your scene partner, do some preliminary work so that you have something to do at your first rehearsal.

First. Using the dialogue your teacher has assigned, write three different scenarios. Make them as different from each other as you can, but try to base each scene on an event that you have some experience with, or that you can project yourself into. If you go too far out in left field, you'll have trouble connecting to the characters and situation you create. Avoid stereotypes, fantasy, comedy, and characters that are much older, much younger, or of a different sex than you are.

Figure out who the characters are and what is happening to make them say these words. Let your mind speculate about what could be going on. Think up more than three ideas, and discard the most obvious ones. Search for creative opportunities within the words.

When you write your scenarios, make sure that you establish the following things for each one:

1. who each of the characters is;
2. what their present and past relationship to each other is;
3. where they are;
4. what happens throughout the scene moment by moment.

Be careful that you establish a linked sequence of actions here, so that each thing that happens causes the next thing to happen. The main problem that you'll run into in these scenes is that you will have a dynamite beginning and a solid ending, but the causal sequence of actions in the middle may be fuzzy and undifferentiated.

A good way to tackle this problem is to decide where the scene starts (A & B are married) and where it ends (A & B decide to get divorced). Then, for each pair of lines in the scene, figure out a step in the sequence from married to divorced.

Second. Memorize your lines before your first rehearsal. Make sure you are word-perfect. Memorize your partner's lines, too.

After you've created three scenarios and sets of characters that you can relate to, it's time to go into rehearsal. Remember to

1. keep the intention clear,
2. make the conflict important to both people,
3. create characters that you could conceivably play (not too old, too young, other sex, bizarre illness, abstract being, etc.),
4. make it "live" for the audience on a moment to moment basis.
5. You must use the words in this scene. You cannot add or change any words. You may, however, have periods of nonverbal communication (a look, touching your partner's shoulder, a hug, slamming down a book in anger, walking away, etc.).

CONTENTLESS SCENE—2-PERSON VERSIONS
(choose version #1 or version #2)
(read **down** for either, not **across**)

version #1	**version #2**
A: Oh! I wasn't expecting you.	A: Want to go out?
B: Why not?	B: Why?
A: Never mind.	A: No reason.
B: Let's talk.	B: I thought so.
A: Okay.	A: Did you?
B: You first.	B: Yes.
A: It's difficult.	A: Let's talk.
B: Tell me.	B: Do we really need to?
A: How long has it been?	A: Yes.
B: Too long.	B: You first.
A: I know.	A: No.
B: I don't think you do.	B: You're being silly.
A: Don't be silly.	A: Never mind.
B: I'm not.	B: Tell me.
A: I know.	A: How long has it been?
B: Do you?	B: I don't know.
A: Yes.	A: Ask me.
B: Suppose I agree.	B: What?
A: Yes.	A: Ask me.
B: No, you tell me.	B: You know I can't.
A: Why?	A: Do I?
B: Because I asked.	B: Let's go out.

CONTENTLESS SCENE—3-PERSON VERSION

(do both columns of lines)

A: Oh! I wasn't expecting you.

B: Why not?

A: Never mind.

C: Let's talk.

A: Okay.

B: You first.

C: It's difficult.

B: Tell me.

C: How long has it been?

B: Too long.

A: I know.

B: I don't think you do.

C: Don't be silly.

B: How long has it been?

C: You know.

B: Do I?

A: Suppose I do.

B: Yes

A: No, you tell me.

C: Why?

A: Because I asked.

C: You can't be serious.

A: Why not?

B: I thought so.

C: Did you?

A: Did you?

B: Yes.

A: Let's go.

C: Didn't they tell you?

B: No.

C: Ask me.

A: What?

C: Ask me.

B: I can't.

A: How long has it been?

C: Too long.

The Basics of Acting

To get an idea of what an actor does—what the actor's job is—look at the word "actor" itself. An actor is "one who acts"—someone who *does*; who sets out to accomplish something; who works toward a goal.

Good acting is active; the good actor does things, makes choices, finds interesting behavioral options. The good actor finds ways to take action, ways that reveal his or her character clearly. This technique gives the good actor a solid, yet flexible base for the role as it develops.

Bad acting is passive; the poor or untrained actor tries to portray emotion, which will always seem fake. One ironclad rule about acting and emotion: Emotion is never a *goal*—it is always the *result* of either achieving or failing to achieve an intention. If an actor commits to and determinedly pursues a character's intention, real emotion will result. They won't have to pretend anything. The passive actor doesn't know how to figure out what the character is trying to do, and thus has to rely on "instinct" to figure out what the character is feeling. Unfortunately, instinct is often just another name for guess-work; there's no way to harness it and make it work for you. The poor (passive actor) has no technique and therefore doesn't DO anything, so the audience can't tell what is going on with the character.

HOW TECHNIQUE HELPS

Learning to act is a lot like learning to play a musical instrument or basketball. You have to learn the basics—the notes, rhythm, dynamics, or how to shoot, dribble, and rebound, or how to choose what your character does—before you can interpret Mozart, sink a sky hook, or play Juliet or Romeo.

There are some simple tasks that you can apply to any character in any play. These tasks help you decide what your character does in the play. These tasks also help you fit your character into the action of the whole play and into the web of character relationships within it.

If you are to be an exciting actor and not a passive performer of stereotypes, you will need command over **Intention**, **Obstacle**, and **Stakes**, and you will need to be aware of the **Biographical Analysis** and the **Given Circumstances**. These tasks, the basic elements of acting, are derived from the work of Constantin Stanislavski.[1] These basics have been used by acting professionals (in one form or another) all over the globe for almost a hundred years. Once you master intention and obstacle and can put them into operation skillfully, you will be well on your way toward being a strong and exciting actor, not a passive and boring one. Once you master Behavioral Analysis and Given Circumstances, you will be equipped to make intelligent and interesting choices concerning intention and obstacle. We briefly discussed these terms in the first chapter, but it is time now to take a more detailed look.

The more you know about the character, the more intelligent and creative you can be in making interesting choices for rehearsal and performance to enhance the "life" of the character. These choices come as you work the role; that means that you build on what the script tells you, the interchanges you

---

Stanislavski was a director and acting teacher in Russia at the end of the 19th century and the beginning of this one. His work was notable and influential because he gave actors a system to represent characters in a much more natural and realistic way than they had ever performed before. His books on acting are still an excellent source for acting students. You can find them in your library.

have with your partner as you rehearse, and the feedback which you get from your director or your classmates in preview performances.

Every day you make choices about what you will do to accomplish with the things you want or need to do during that day. You are constantly faced with many options. Any one of these options will lead you down a path with other possibilities and more options. So you weigh the best decision as you consider your choices. Shall I go to the bank before I go to class? If I do, I might be late for class. What will happen in that case? Or shall I go to the bank after class? If I do, I may be too late to catch my friend at the student union. If I don't, I may risk bouncing a check!

Actors read the script to see what choices the characters make throughout the course of the play. The actor constantly asks: How do the choices my character makes bring me closer to where I want to go? But it goes deeper than that. You will get the opportunity to make lots of choices which are not specifically in the script, but which come from your own understanding of the character's needs and behavior patterns. This is where the fun of acting comes in. This is why no two performances are ever alike. Yes, you must be true to the script and to the director's interpretation of that script, but you will get to make hundreds of choices as to how the character gets from the beginning of the play to the ending.

Intention

The word "intention" points you to a goal. It is the thing the character wants; the goal. If you "intend" to do something, then all of your efforts will be brought toward accomplishing that goal. Your desires, wants, and needs determine what trajectory your actions will take. In actors' language, your "intention" is what you want to do. (Please note that it is sometimes called by other terms: Motivation, Objective, Goal, Victory, etc. For the purpose of simplicity, we will stick with the term "intention" in this text.)

Personal Intention Since most plays are based on real life, it should be no surprise to you that the intentions which drive a character in a drama are quite similar to the intentions you yourself have in life. We have all learned how setting personal goals help us to focus our "doing" and allow us to keep on the path which gets us to the objective, the goal we set. What goals do you have? (Personal, financial, spiritual, social, physical, etc.) Look at the samples below and then jot down a couple for yourself:

> I want to graduate from college with a degree.
> I want to marry and raise a family.
> I want to play the accordion for parties.
> I want to get along with my roommates.
> I want to make friends with everyone I meet.
> I want to date _____.
> I want to pay off my college expenses.

My own personal goals for this year:

1. I want to _____.
2. I want to _____.

My own personal goals for the next five years:

3. I want to _____.
4. I want to _____.

Notice that each of the goals in the model is in active verb form—"I want TO PAY OFF, TO GRADUATE, TO MARRY, etc. These words give us specific actions to DO to achieve those goals. Therefore, the goals are measured by the activity which takes us there.

Try to do the same with the personal goals you have listed above expressing forward movement in the "plot" of your life. Put these goals in strong active verb form. (That means avoiding the words "be" or "become.") Continue to adjust the intentions you have written above as you check out the following basic rules in selecting an intention:

1. Choose strong and vital verbs. Instead of saying "I want to be a Senior next year," say "I want to nail my classes this year" or "I want to pass with flying colors." Make sure that you have an active verb which follows "I want" in the sentence. Instead of saying: "I want my parents to respect me," say, "I want to convince my parents of my character and integrity."
2. Try to pin down the specific action it will take to accomplish your goal. Instead of saying, "I want to have money," say "I want to get a fabulous job and invest wisely."
3. Don't get too grandiose, but try to capture your real need. Instead of "I want to achieve self-fulfillment," say "I want to look in the mirror every morning and like who I see."
4. Choose an intention that directly acts upon others. Say "I want to inspire a legitimate Hollywood producer to request me for the lead in his movie." Don't say "I want to be a famous actor/actress." That is too passive.

Notice that specific word choice is very important here. We try to pick the very best words to express our deepest desires. Think carefully about active verbs/specific modifiers/direct objects (i.e., "nail," "fabulous," and "producer") as you try to pin down what action it would take to accomplish your goals. (There will be more on the topic of how important word choices are in Chapter 10.)

Character Intention Since most plays and real life are so much alike, seeing the similarities between your personal goals and those of a character is not difficult. In fact, the world of the play is less complicated than real life. In a play, the events are simplified to reveal only a portion of a character's life. This is necessary for cohesiveness in the plot, so the play doesn't take a lifetime to perform! However, this simplification of plot makes selecting an intention for the character much easier, since the action of the play will focus on only one portion of this character's needs or goals.

But whether the play is a simplified version of life or not, the intention a character has in a play is without a doubt the most important piece of information you as an actor can have about the role you play. Everything the character does, all his or her choices, each of his or her actions, is connected to that intention. Your knowledge about what the intention is drives all your subsequent choices and decisions about the life and action of your character.

Thus, the first question you ask when you approach a role is "What does my character ultimately want to do or get?". The answer to this question is the character's **intention** for the play. When you approach a role, first read the play and list all of the possibilities for your character's intentions. (Remember to keep your answer to the question in active verb form.) You will eventually pick just one, but it helps to get all possibilities in front of you before you settle on the perfect intention for the role. Sometimes there is a dual intention; i.e., *"My character wants to save the family fortune and find true love."* If both of these things are equally important to the character and the plot, there is no reason to separate them. But analyze carefully.

Let's return to the example of playing the character of Romeo in the play *Romeo and Juliet* by Shakespeare. After reading the play you know that Romeo **does** the following things:

he bemoans the loss of his former girlfriend;
he goes to a party to forget the girlfriend;
he falls for a new girl;
he arranges to meet with her secretly;
he marries the girl;
he tries to prevent a fight between her family and his;
he accidentally kills one of her family;

he runs away;
he goes back to see her;
he finds out that she is dead;
he decides to kill himself to be with her;
he buys poison and goes to her in her tomb;
he kills himself at her side.

It is worth thinking about some of your work in acting as though you were a detective. You have the play to work with. The play is your evidence. And in it, in its dialogue, stage directions, setting notes, even in its prop lists, are the basic information from which you will develop your character. You have already discovered that just saying dialogue out loud in your own voice and person is not acting. Somewhere between when you are assigned a role and when you do an actual performance lies a lot of discovery and investigation on your part.

Now it's time to be a detective. What holds this role together? Let's work with Romeo. What does Romeo want to do throughout the play? What constant force or goal keeps him on the track that leads through all of these steps to the final action of the play? In other words, what is Romeo's **intention?**

Here are some possibilities for Romeo's intention:

1. to be happy (too passive)
2. to find love (too general; doesn't include anyone else directly)
3. to go to bed with Juliet (too short term)
4. to escape from the pressures of his family (doesn't include a great deal of the important action of the play)
5. to settle down with a woman who loves him (doesn't include the greatness of his need or struggle)
6. to love a girl who will love him unconditionally (now we're getting somewhere)

This is by no means an exhaustive list. Every actor will see different things in a role and will bring new insights to his analysis. That's just fine! If you and your best friend were both to do the role of Romeo, you can be sure that each of you would have different insights into the role, based on experience, sensitivity, philosophical views, etc. The "right" intention is one that follows the script, incorporates your own insights, and completely illustrates the behavior of the character.

Review: Points to Consider When Choosing an Intention

1. Some general rules for articulating the intention:
   a. Keep the intention in active verb form. Don't use the construction "to be ___."
      EXAMPLE: to gain power over all members of the firm;
      NOT: to be rich and powerful.
   b. Try to pin down the specific action of the character, keeping in mind all that he or she does in the play.
      EXAMPLE: to find the person who hurt my friends;
      NOT: to discover the truth.
   c. Try to capture the real need of the character. (Don't choose the too general or all-encompassing verb.)
      EXAMPLE: to regain approval from the members of my family;
      NOT: to justify myself.
   d. Choose an intention that directly acts upon others.
      EXAMPLE: to make everyone in this room bow down to me;
      NOT: to achieve greatness.

2. Picking the right verb will help you keep on track as you develop your role. Here are some good active verbs to keep in mind when you are choosing your intention for a character:

grasp	hold
win	force
maintain	destroy
build	solve
create	resolve

Do you see how powerful these words are? They have a great potential for action and forward movement in the script. Develop a list of your own.

3. Make sure you've picked the best intention. The way to be sure is to periodically go back to the text and look at the action of the character to see if everything still fits. If you suspect that your intention may not be the strongest choice, then rethink it. Hold the intention you chose up against the evidence of the text and the discoveries you made in rehearsal about the character's relationships. Your new discoveries may help you to redefine the intention—to make it more specific, more applicable to relationships, more active, or more in line with the larger needs of the character. It's not a sin to adjust your intention as you work the role; the best actors hone the intention throughout the rehearsal process.

4. Don't worry if your intentions seem vague at first. This part of the acting technique takes practice. You will get better at finding a strong intention every time you do a role. In the meantime, practice your intention-selection skills on your own: every time you read a play or novel, or see a movie or a play, pick out intentions for each of the characters. Every time you set out to do something in your own life, try to state your intention, using the guidelines outlined above.

Obstacles

What you want to achieve is called your intention. What stands in the way of your achieving that intention is called your obstacle. How often do you get what you want? Do you ever run into a problem which prevents you from achieving an important goal? Of course, we all have that experience. It's part of life to deal with hassles of one kind or another. We do not live in a perfect world.

What gets in the way of what you want to do? What hurdles do you have to climb over to achieve your goal? These are the **obstacles** to your intention. Identifying them can help you know what to do, moment to moment, day to day, to achieve each intention in your own life.

Personal Obstacles Go back to the personal intentions you listed for yourself. Think of all the events, people, circumstances, and personal shortcomings that could prevent each intention from happening. Here are the samples and possible obstacles for these intentions.

I want to graduate from college with a degree in _____.

OBSTACLES:
party too much
can't pass Math I
don't enjoy my major
do poorly in writing

I want to pay off my college expenses.

OBSTACLES:
no time for a part-time job during school
can't control my spending habits
parents have no money to help out
don't like to save money

Notice that each of these obstacles is an actual hurdle to overcome, not just a vague personal problem. As long as you have goals (intentions) for your life, you will have events or circumstances to hurdle (i.e., obstacles to overcome). Fortunately for us, we seldom confront one obstacle after another as characters do in a play.

Internal and External Obstacles   Notice also that some of the obstacles listed above are internal and some are external. The internal obstacles are the ones which literally come from inside you. They are within you and are a part of your own nature. Internal obstacles may be from some part of your habitual nature, patterns of thinking, or other personal limitations. For example, "party too much" could really be a lack of willpower or inability on your own part to say "No!" to a friend. With internal obstacles, the adjustment has to be made inside ourselves, not with outside circumstances or someone else. It's a valuable life lesson when we recognize that the place to begin in removing the obstacles of life is with ourselves!

Conversely, some of the above obstacles are external. These are obstacles which lie outside ourselves; these are the ones beyond our immediate control: i.e., "parents have no money to help out." External obstacles can be controlled by some great entity way beyond our immediate reach; for example, government requirements, bad weather, or high interest rates. But outside obstacles can also be in the shape of other people, too, such as a bully standing in the way of your getting to go to the rest room in the fifth grade.

Now try this with the sample intentions you listed earlier. Pick a couple of the ones you chose and determine what might get in the way of achieving your goals:

Your personal intention #1 or #2:
I want to _____
Obstacles to that intention:
Internal Obstacles: _____

_____

_____

External Obstacles: _____

_____

_____

Your personal intention #3 or #4:
I want to _____.
Obstacles to that intention:
Internal Obstacles: _____

_____

_____

External Obstacles: _____

_____

_____

Character Obstacles   Of course, the process of internal and external obstacles we face in our own lives are quite similar to what characters in plays deal with. If it were not for obstacles, most plays would be pretty dull. Remember: "Drama is conflict."

In drama we love to watch someone struggle with a great obstacle and overcome it. We even receive a kind of understanding (or catharsis) when someone struggles with a great obstacle and loses (as long as they lose with dignity). That's human nature. Nobody would come to plays if nothing challenging happened. Think about it: would you rather watch a slow moving train or an Olympic competition? Why? Which one has more obstacles and more drama? Which one holds our attention? Without clear and significant obstacles, there is no drama.

Once you have determined your character's intention, the second question to ask is "What gets in the way of what your character wants to do?" The answers to this question are the character's obstacles.

How do you pick the obstacles that your character has to face? First, reread the play, reviewing the intention you had in mind. Next, make a list of people, events, circumstances, and personal handicaps that the character has to overcome in order to achieve her intention. Think about all of the outside forces which prevail against the character—these are the external obstacles. Then locate all of the ways in which the personal makeup of the character interferes with what he or she is trying to accomplish. These are the internal obstacles.

Let's go back to Romeo for a moment. His intention is to love a girl who will love him unconditionally. What gets in the way of that? Here are a few things he has to hurdle:

an old girlfriend he can't get over;

friends who think he is a lovesick booby;

parents who disapprove of his new choice of girl;

potential in-laws who hate his guts;

a local civil war partially created by his family;

an incredibly impulsive and passionate nature;

a lack of faith that things will turn out all right.

The internal obstacles are "the impulsive and passionate nature" and "the lack of faith that things will turn out right." The external obstacles are "the parents," "the friends," and "the civil war." Note that "the old girlfriend" is somewhere in the middle: External in the sense that she does not return his love and he cannot do much about how she feels; Internal in the sense that it's his own hang-up (being in love with an untouchable woman) and he needs to "get over it!" It shouldn't surprise you that obstacles don't fall neatly into categories. What in life does? Use your judgment and insights to explore whether obstacles are internal or external. You may not come up with a clean list of each, but you will certainly more fully understand the nature of the particular obstacles!

You will notice that just about everything that happens in this play either furthers Romeo's intention or presents an obstacle to it—that is, Shakespeare's genius and good dramatic structure. A good play makes this whole analytical process much easier.

Analysis

Biographical Analysis   Remember that a good actor is a good detective. Of course, a good detective must do good ground work before drawing final deductions. Therefore, to be a good actor, you too need to be a good investigator. This is where the Who, What, Where, When, Why, and How questions come in handy. Think about the last time you had a crush on someone whom you only saw for a short time or met briefly. Then you ran into someone who knew that person very well. What kind of questions did you ask? What kinds of things did you want to know about them? What categories did you need to fill in to determine whether you were really interested in pursuing this guy or girl? You were doing your research, weren't you?

Well, it's the same with a character you play, whether it's a scene or an entire play. You need to know everything you can about the person, the surrounding events, the environment, etc. Here are some exploration categories with some questions to ask about each and some sample answers. (Note that you would normally do this analysis focusing all your answers on one character in a specific scene. For the purposes of variety, we have used several different characters from Shakespeare's *Romeo and Juliet* for our answers.[2])

1. Biographical (the present)

Name: Has the author given you clues as to the nature of the character? (*'Romeo' derives from the ancient Italian meaning 'Roman' or 'of Rome.' Looking up the meaning of names can often give you valuable information about the character.*) Does the character choose to use a nickname or name other than his or her given name? *Not in this case.* Why?

Sexual Life, Experience, Attitudes: Gender (Male or Female). What about sexual practices, orientation, level of sexual desires, or history? (*Romeo's experience in this area seems limited to a previous girlfriend, whom in the beginning of the play, he has not been able to get over. His ability to fall deeply, romantically in love is a strong force and determines much of what he does in the play.*) Is this a driving factor for the character's actions in the play? (*Absolutely!*)

Age/Maturity Level: Numerical response. (*about 17 to 20. Estimates are OK if the exact age isn't mentioned in the play.*) But how does this person rate when compared with others of his or her own age group? (*Romeo is more romantic than his peer group. He is as impulsive as they are—maybe more so.*) How are they more mature than others? (*Romeo tries to stop the fight between Tybalt and Mercutio, but ultimately joins the fight—with terrible consequences*) Less mature? Why? (*In regard to love, Romeo is far more impulsive and reckless than his peers, which shows immaturity.*)

Physical Appearance (*Notable, distinguishing characteristics; choice/style of clothing*): Basic description as it's given in the script. (*Romeo is young, well-built and handsome, if not "macho" looking.*) Describe the costume in detail (*colors, style, decoration, weapons, shoes, or boots; remember, each detail is a specific choice made by the designer and the director for a reason. Don't assume anything is random.*) How does the character move? (*He moves with passion and certainty, but fights like an athlete. He is both impulsive and gentle.*) Anything unusual?

Education, Intellect, Thinking Abilities: Formal Education? (*Romeo comes from a noble family, so he has been educated in a classical manner, likely by tutors.*) Informal Education? (*Amongst his peers and friends, he has a certain amount of "street cred," because of his ability to fight. But he is also viewed by his peers as too impulsive.*) Basic intellect? (*Romeo is a bright young man, with great determination and passion, but not good at accurately calculating risk factors in his behavior.*) Are there thought patterns which this character tends toward? (*Romeo sees the world in terms of his own needs and is unable to see beyond his own immediate desires.*)

Social and Economic Background, Status (*note: Status is more than the character's "class," but their personal social standing and level of respect among the other characters in the play. Be specific and detailed here.*): How do others look at this character? (*Romeo comes from a wealthy upper class family, but they are well known for being involved in a contentious and troublesome public feud with another noble family. He is the one who makes the decisions about his love life, though his parents would have to approve; however, Juliet is betrothed to another, in a marriage arrangement set up by her parents*). Who are this person's friends? (*Romeo's friends are Mercutio, Friar Lawrence, Benvolio, Balthazar.*) Assets? (*Wealthy parents*) Debits? (*His family has a reputation as troublesome.*)

Emotional Characteristics, Typical Mood: (*At the beginning of the play, Romeo is melancholy over a lost girlfriend. Joyful when he falls in love with Juliet.*) Normally stable? (*fairly stable, but impulsive*) Any difficult conflicts between the character's desires/needs and the circumstances? (*He desires/needs Juliet, but she is already promised to Paris.*) How does this character handle stress? (*with risky and impulsive behavior*)

General Personality: (*use your own judgment here*) How would you describe this person to a casting director? What elements of the personality stand out? Which of the above are the key points to consider in developing a full picture of the person? What else is important to understand about them?

Given Circumstances   Given circumstances are just as important in character analysis as is biographical information. The Given Circumstances are all the information about the scene, the world of the play. They have an impact on the actions and even the intentions of the characters. Knowing as much as you can about this world enables you to intelligently select the best choices for your character to make. The principle elements within given circumstances include the following.

Present Locale and Situation: Weather? (*in some scripts, this is very important—don't overlook it*) Locale? (*In Romeo and Juliet the locale is Verona, Italy.*)

Time of day? (*List times when your chosen scene takes place. You can simply put general terms like "morning" or "evening."*) Situation? (*Try to summarize the situation in a few sentences. Do not try to include all plot details. Example: 'Romeo is in love with Juliet, who is promised to Paris. Romeo forms a plan to overcome the many obstacles to marrying her, but many things go wrong'. In a chosen scene, you would describe the specific information for that scene.*)

Earlier Experiences or Situations of Note: Factors which may have contributed to the nature of this character? (*The feud that his family has been involved with for many years.*) Relationships with siblings or parents? (*his relationship with his parents is affected by the feud—they would never support his marriage to Juliet.*) Previous experiences which determine how the character reacts to the current circumstances? (*He is very hurt by losing his previous girlfriend.*)

Actions Immediately Preceding the Scene: (*Important actions taken by the character*) Events leading up to the conflict in the play? What just happened which makes this scene inevitable?

Reading the Script   By now you are realizing how much information is available to you from the script. The details which can become very important in determining how a character would behave in a situation can come directly from information you get from what the character says, what the character does, what he says about others, and what others say about him or her.

Whenever you work a role, read your script carefully; reread it several times keeping these questions and categories in mind. Many professional actors insist on reading their scripts daily in order to keep coming up with insights and understand their characters better.

CHAPTER TWO EXERCISES

1. To understand the importance of "doing" or taking action (as opposed to just "feeling" an emotion) try this:
   a. Sit in a chair facing your partner, and without doing anything (don't make any faces, don't move, don't say anything, or breathe aloud), "be" angry, or happy, or sad, or impatient. Remember, you can't move or do anything at all.
   b. Ask your partner what emotion you are feeling. Ask how he knew (or did not know).
   c. Now take your shoe off. Put it on again as if you are getting ready to go out with someone you really like to do something interesting and unusual and you can't wait to get started—like visiting the new gorilla baby at the zoo, or trying on expensive shoes, or driving your best friend's father's Maserati.
   d. Ask your scene partner what emotion you are feeling. Ask how he knew.

2. To practice intention and obstacle:
   a. Partner up with a person from the class. You are roommates or siblings or lovers. You each have a clear intention and the other person is the obstacle. Improvise this scene for three minutes.
   b. Discuss what happened. Apply the vocabulary we've learned by applying the terminology: What was your intention? What were your obstacles? Your Given Circumstances?
   Sample: Given Circumstances: #2 has borrowed a sweater from #1. They are roommates and friends. This scene takes place in the late afternoon in their apartment. The sweater is new and flattering to both.
   Intention #1: To get your sweater back so you can wear it for photo sitting.
   Intention #2: To wear the sweater on a date with a new love this evening.
   Obstacles? Friendship for other person, other person's desire to wear sweater, conflict of date and photo sitting happening at the same time, selfishness of other person, etc.

3. Character exercises. Work on the following exercise as a means of connecting action and given circumstance:
   a. You and a partner each select a character to perform from a scene you have been assigned in class. Develop an improvised scene of these two people engaged in a situation not specifically in the play, e.g., Character A and Character B talking about extreme weather they have experienced; Character A and Character B talking about how to take care of horses; Character A and Character B talking about the value of education; Character A and Character B talking about moral behavior in their day and age.
   b. Be certain to have each character play a clear intention, but also make sure that your characters talk, act, and respond in ways consistent with what goes on in the rest of the actual play.
   c. After you have rehearsed the improvised scene a few times, perform it for the class. Then have the rest of the class discuss with the two of you how well and how much what you did in the scene was "in character." That is, get a critique of how well you stayed within the given circumstances of the play in this improvised situation.

4. Art Gallery exercises for Intention/Obstacle/Given Circumstances: Set this up in your classroom, as follows:

   Given Circumstances: The Art Gallery is opening and everyone is able to come and go as they please. The walls are full of interesting paintings and there are benches for patrons to rest on. There is one guard on duty.

   a. Each person comes in with a particular intention (i.e., to find a place to rest my feet for a while). Explore the obstacles which you can create for yourself. Do not interchange with others yet.

   b. Same as above, but you must strengthen both the intention and the obstacle.
   (You may change if the ones you chose didn't work so well.)

   b. Same as above, but you may interact with the others in the scene to achieve your intention. Be aware of all of the new obstacles provided by the other people in the improvisation.

   Teacher's Note: Keep side-coaching during the improv and debrief to determine the intentions and experiences of the students. It's helpful if there are no more than 10 onstage for each round; the others will learn a lot by trying to identify intentions, obstacles, etc.

5. Applying Intention, Obstacle, and Analysis to a Character Analysis format:

   a. Fill out the following form for a role in "Blonds." (You will find the entire script in the Appendix.) If you are a male, do Marty's role. If you are a female, do Susan's. Go step by step and do some serious thinking and research in the script. This is your chance to be a detective. Read it carefully a couple of times.

   b. Sit down in a quiet place where you can concentrate on your character exclusively and fill out the form. It's a good idea to establish the habit of writing in pencil, because as you go through rehearsals you will understand things more completely and need to change your mind.

   c. There may be items you still don't know the answers; if so, go back to the script and make sure that you didn't overlook a valuable clue. If what you are looking for is not there, then sit back and think about the other bits of information that you do have. You may be able to abstract the information you are seeking from the information that you already have. You will be surprised at how much you know about your character.

CHARACTER ANALYSIS

(for class discussion on "Blonds")

Name: _____

Character you are playing: _____

Title of play: _____

Author of play: _____

    A. Basic Analysis

        1. Biographical (the present)
           Name:

           Sexual Life, Experience, Attitudes:

           Age, Maturity Level:

           Physical Appearance (Notable, distinguishing characteristics;
           choice/style of clothing):

           Education, Intellect, Thinking Abilities:

           Social and Economic Background, Status:

           Emotional Characteristics, Typical Mood:

           General Personality:

2. Given Circumstances (pre-existing and existing conditions that affect his or her behavior)

Present Locale and Situation:

Earlier Experiences or Situations of Note:

Actions Immediately Preceding This Scene:

B. Behavior and Goals
Intention for the play:

Intention for the scene:

Obstacles:
Internal

External

Relationship and Emotion

RELATIONSHIP

In real life, whenever we speak or do something, we are interacting with another person or persons—even if it is only in our own mind (talking to ourselves, another person, or God). Everything we do has an effect on someone else. We don't act or speak without targeting someone else with our actions or thoughts.

Think about it: how many lives have you touched today? Your boss, your co-workers, your teacher, your roommates, your parents, your siblings, or your significant other are the obvious ones. But what about the person who sold you coffee? The guy who was on the opposite side of the intersection you stopped at on the way to work or school? The telemarketer who called last night while you were having dinner? You affect these persons' lives with your words and actions too. Maybe the effect is smaller—but maybe not! Suppose you hadn't seen the stop light; then your impact on the guy on the other side of the intersection could have been more than minimal. Suppose you realized that the person who sold you coffee this morning might be the next great love of your life? Suppose the telemarketer only needed to sell one more magazine subscription to make her National Telemarketer of the Month?

By the same token, other people's words and actions can affect us. Since this process is reciprocal, we need to consider others' actions and thoughts as we interact with them. There are times, in fact, when we get overloaded and crave isolation from the constant dealing with others. (Margaret puts it this way in *The Lady's Not for Burning* by Christopher Fry: "I could do with a splendid vacation in a complete vacuum!") Mostly, however, we need other people to bounce ideas off, to get help from, to play with, to work with, to confirm our convictions, to validate our beliefs, etc.

Working with or Against the Partner

Just as you need to consider others' actions and thoughts in your life, when you act you have to consider the other characters as you plot the road toward the intention. Characters in a play don't operate in a vacuum either.

In acting, we call this other person the *partner* because without him or her, the scene cannot take place! This person has the potential of helping you. That is why you are there in the scene with this person—she could be the one to help you get what you want! If you can circumvent the partner's objections (obstacles) and get her on your side, you will achieve your intention.

Therefore, part of the job of acting is to figure out whether the other characters involved in your scene will be a help or a hindrance in achieving your intention. "How can this person help me achieve my goal?" "How could this person get in my way?" Once you have answered these questions you will be able to figure out what to DO to this person, with this person, or in spite of this person to get you to your goal.

Let's go back to the earlier personal example from Chapter 2. The intention was to graduate from college. This seemingly independent goal directly affects several people (parents, bank managers, employers, teachers, friends) when you consider what is necessary to remedy the lack of necessary money (obstacle). "How could my parents help me get the money I need?" "How could they get in my way?" "How could the bank manager help me get the money?" "How could he prevent it?" and so on.

Now try this with your sample intentions. Pick one of the intention/obstacle sets you chose in the previous chapter and determine who might help or hurt you in achieving your goal:

Your personal intention #1 or #2:

I want to _____

Obstacles to that intention:

Internal Obstacles: _____

_____

External obstacles: _____

_____

_____

People who could help: _____

    How? _____

    Another person _____

    How? _____

People who could hinder: _____

    How? _____

    Another person _____

    How? _____

Partners in the Scene

As you search for intention and obstacles, you will find direct ways to influence the behavior of the other characters in your scenes. You won't passively wait for them to do something to you; that would make for a pretty dull production! You will actively try to perceive:

1. whether they help you get your goal or stand in your way;
2. if you can get them to do what you need them to do in order to achieve your intention.

Whether the person is a helper or a hindrance, he or she is called the partner—the one whose behavior you are trying to influence. Remember that the other character also has an intention and is trying to use a tactic on you too. So YOU are the partner of the other character's actions.

Let's apply this to our example from *Romeo and Juliet*. How much does Romeo's intention (to love a girl who will love him unconditionally) involve other people? In order to achieve his goal, he will need to influence the lives of at least the following people: Juliet, all of her family, his own parents and relatives, his buddies, the Friar, Juliet's kindly nurse, the guy who wants to marry Juliet, and even the ruler of the town! That's quite a list of people! Now, if you were playing Romeo, you would analyze each scene in terms of the partner(s) of the scene and how each would help or hurt you in your love quest.

How does each help?:

Juliet	all of her family
Romeo's parents/relatives	Mercutio
Balthasar	the Friar
Juliet's nurse	Paris
the ruler of the town	

How does each hurt?:

Juliet	all of her family
Romeo's parents/relatives	Mercutio
Balthasar	the Friar
Juliet's nurse	Paris
the ruler of the town	

The beauty of this system is that you will have someone specific to focus on and something concrete to do whenever you analyze and then tackle a scene.

Stop—Look and Listen

If you act with and try to influence your partner strongly you will find yourself listening carefully for signs of success, searching for clues of failure, and being taken aback by new information given to you. Treat each partner as your character's lifeline to achieving your intention.

How do you do this? The most important way is to listen. Think about what the partner is telling you or doing to you. Evaluate all new information from the partner in terms of your intention. Watch your partner. Be on the lookout for new obstacles that he may throw at you or for new ways that might work to influence him.

Let's take an example from real life. You are a female in your twenties and you want to ask a guy named Cameron out on a date. You see him downtown looking in a store window. Intention: to get Cameron to go out with you. You say, "Hi!" He says, "Hi!" You try to hear in that "Hi" whether he is glad to see you or not. You chat for a while; all the while you are checking out his face and body language to see if he is warming up to you. You finally get around to asking the question, "Are you doing anything Friday night?" You listen very carefully because Cameron could come back with any one of a number of responses:

"Yes, I'm going to the city with my girlfriend."

"No, but I need to clean my room."

"Well, I might be free. Let me check my calendar and get back to you."

"Why do you ask?"

"No, I'm not busy Friday. Would you like to do something together?"

Listening carefully lets you know where you stand in relation to your intention. That's how you detect obstacles or find reinforcement in pursuing the action you have begun.

By the same token, visual cues can tell you a great deal about the potential success or failure of your goal. Looking at your potential date carefully will reveal a lot. Is he smiling at you as you talk? Is it a polite smile or a "I want to know you better" smile? Is he looking around for an excuse to leave or is he hoping the bus won't come and spoil the moment? Is he fixing his hair or straightening his clothing? (That's a good sign!)

One more time: Listen! Really listen; don't pretend to listen. Look! Really see; don't just pretend to see.

EMOTION

Up until now, we haven't talked much about emotion. The only mention has been in connection with choosing Romeo's intention—one of the ones we considered didn't include the greatness of his need or struggle. One of the reasons people come to the theatre or go to the movies is to see someone deal with the great frustrations of life. It's called "empathy" and it's what connects us to another's experiences.

Human emotions are part of the price—and pay-off—for being human. Important emotional things happen in all our lives, because they're part of being alive. A very important part of acting is sharing your real human experience with others, so that they can understand their lives and experiences better. What are some of the emotional landmarks of your life so far?

What was your happiest moment? _____

What was your saddest moment? _____

What was your proudest moment? _____

What was your most fearful moment? _____

Put these memories in your back pocket. They are a part of you and will help you understand the characters you play.

Emotions and Intentional Acting

There is a rule here for actors that ALWAYS applies: Emotion is never a GOAL—it is always a RESULT. Good actors rely upon the action of the scene to feed them the emotions. Remember that the action is determined by the character's intention and the tactics necessary to circumvent the obstacles. The emotions that result from a focus on what the character is trying to do in the scene will be far more real, complex, and powerful than any emotions that an actor could fake.

So often, beginning actors think that acting is mainly the expression of emotion. They don't realize (until they start to work at acting as a skilled craft) that emotion is the result of action, not vice versa. Here's how it works: Emotion naturally results when the action is completed, frustrated, or transformed. For example, you get angry or anxious when you are trying to open the door and it is stuck for no good reason. Your action (to open the door) is frustrated and so you get angry with the door (or your inability to open it) or anxious that you won't be able to get in or out.

In much the same way, you become happy or relieved when you pass your course final. Your intention (to pass the class) is completed and so you become happy that you have succeeded and relieved that you won't have to take the class over. You get embarrassed when you are sitting down in a chair and it breaks underneath you. Your intention (to sit down) has been changed (to keep from falling down, or to look as if you meant to fall down) and so you get embarrassed (i.e., feel foolish for not anticipating the course of events).

Playing the Emotions—A No-No

It is a deadly mistake to play the emotions of a scene instead of playing the action. This mistake will cost you the moment-to-moment life of the scene and its believability. Stick with your intention and watch out for the obstacles instead. The emotions will come along automatically, they'll be the appropriate ones, and you won't have to fake anything.

1. Playing emotions is too general. If you play emotions, the audience will know that something is causing you to feel angry or frightened or happy, etc., but they won't be able to tell what the details of the circumstances are.

2. Playing emotions feels good to an actor, but leaves the audience empty. We love to watch someone fight and win (or fight and lose, for that matter), but we don't enjoy watching someone get off on their own emotions. It seems self-indulgent and selfish.
3. Playing emotions puts you inside yourself. That means that your partner is getting very little from you. And if the partner is getting very little, then the audience will get even less.

Doing and Emotions

The right way is to *do*. Then you will *feel*. That's what intentional acting is all about. Your emotions will naturally connect, in a much more truthful way, if you focus on your intention, listen to your partner, and keep alert for obstacles.

Remember: You can't tell anything about anybody's feelings if they sit motionless on a chair. You can only tell what people are feeling by what they do and how they do it. This is true of people in real life as well as of characters in plays. You decide about other people based on what they do and say (talking is an action, too). You can never reliably tell what people are thinking in their minds or feeling in their hearts until they DO something.

Emotional Truth

We all relate to human experience. We recognize feelings, emotions in the lives of others and attempt to put them into our own frame of reference. (For example, if you hear of a friend who has fallen in love, you are reminded of how it felt when you first fell in love.) The stories we remember and respond to are those whose emotions we recognize because we have experienced these emotions ourselves.

Life continues to make us grow and to educate us emotionally. If you haven't yet known someone who has died, stick around for a while: you will. If you haven't fallen in love, stick around for a while: you will. If you haven't had a broken heart, stick around for a while: you will.

In much the same way we all recognize truly represented human experience on the stage or screen. Audiences recognize whether you're telling them "emotional truth." Watch for it in your classmates; you'll know it when you see it.

The bolder you are in your choices, and the more truthful you are in relating to your character and your partner in the scene, the more strongly the audience will be affected. If you reveal your feelings truthfully, the audience will respond, because you have made them understand not only your experience and emotions, but experiences and emotions from their lives, too.

One more *"no-no"*: Don't fall into the trap of "describing" a feeling. It is impossible to *ACT* an adjective or an adverb! *Loud, soft, big, small* are modifiers; *angrily, stupidly, happily, aggressively* are descriptions, but none of this will lead you to an honest emotion. By themselves, they are empty. Remember: a truthful emotion comes only from gaining an intention, or failing to gain it. Again, emotion is a result of *ACTION*, of *doing*. Real emotion will not result from a "description." Stay away from adjectives or adverbs, and stick with *actions*.

"AS IFS" FOR YOUR CHARACTER

One way to "get inside your character," as directors often say, is to find a parallel experience which you have had, or one which you can easily relate to, to help you understand the given circumstances the person is dealing with. Actors call the parallel experience the AS IF—or, as Stanislavski called it, the "Particularization." Read your character's situation, goals, and actions "AS IF" it were happening to you.

If your character is drug addicted and wants desperately to stop, you need put yourself into a situation which makes you feel and act "as if" you were a person fighting drug addiction. What personal experiences do you have which can be brought to bear on this?

Have you experienced drug, or alcohol, or cigarette, or food, or pornography, or video game addiction? If you have, then you have an "as if" to help you understand.

Have you fought a bad habit (procrastination, credit card spending, gambling, etc.) and experienced the helplessness which comes when you find yourself doing the very thing you said you would never do again? If you have, there's your "as if."

Have you found yourself in a behavior pattern you swore you never would fall into again (i.e., going out with a guy or girl who doesn't respect you, but is exciting to be with)? You've got the makings of the "as if."

Get used to investigating your life (or those you are close to) for these circumstances which help you to relate to the experience and feelings of the characters you play. If you pursue acting and view everything as potential meat for the performing grist, you may find yourself in a situation like the following true scenario:

> "We were having a brutal fight—verbally abusing each other and refusing to take the blame for anything. As he looked at me with anger and doubt in his eyes, I saw that the relationship was disintegrating quickly. And in my head, the actress part of me said, 'I've got to remember this conflict and the feeling of loss. It's exactly what's missing in the second to last scene in *Loose Ends*!' "

Now that's taking it a bit far, but you get the point. If we want to portray life as it is, we need to be aware of life and live it!

STAKES

A useful and very important term we use in discussing advocacy and commitment in acting is the word **stakes**. *Stakes can be defined as the extent or degree to which a character wants to achieve an intention.* We borrow the term from general usage and specifically from gambling—perhaps an apt metaphor.

Two people are playing cards and have placed money on the table as a bet—winner take all. Each of them wants to win the hand of cards just dealt. As they each withdraw extra cards from the deck, how badly do they want to win? Well, how high are the stakes? If they are college students and have each invested 25 cents on the game, the stakes are pretty low. It is not very important for either of them to win. Drawing the extra cards and the energy they put into trying to win are not very important to them. The stakes are low.

Now let's raise the stakes. Suppose they have each put $500.00 on the table, and also suppose this $500.00 is for each of them their rent and spending money for the whole month. Now, how badly does each of them want to achieve their intention—winning the card game and collecting the pot? The higher the stakes, the more they are committed to achieving their intention, and the greater the extent they want to win.

In plays and in acting, the stakes are seldom so literal as money on the table, but there are stakes for every character in every play, nonetheless. How badly does Juliet want to love Romeo and be with him? Badly enough that she is willing to kill herself if she can't have him. How badly does George in *Of Mice and Men* want to keep his dim-witted buddy, Lennie, from harm? Badly enough that he would kill his friend before letting people send Lennie to prison. Those are very high stakes! And any actors playing any of those roles would have done both the play and us a great disservice if they failed to make the stakes as high as called for in the play.

Making the stakes high involves two jobs for the actor: realizing how high the stakes are for the character in the play, and making specific actor choices to show to the audience through your performance the extent of the stakes for the character you are playing. The goal of your character must be so important that he or she would do nearly anything to achieve it.

The extent and degree of the stakes for a character are generally discovered in a play by looking at: 1. what actions the character is willing to take to achieve her intention, and 2. the amount of time or effort the character spends in attempting to achieve the intention—this effort is seen in the actions the character does, as well as in what the character says. To use another play example, Willie Loman in *Death of a Salesman* talks throughout the play—nearly in every scene—about how he wants to earn love and respect from his sons. It becomes obvious the stakes are pretty high for Willie, since he talks about achieving that intention all the time. But it is also clear the stakes are really high for him when one looks at his action in the play. He struggles in scene after scene to get others to respect him. Nothing seems to work. Finally, near the end of the play, Willie kills himself, hoping that this final action (and the insurance money the family will get because of his death) will earn him his sons' respect at last.

Certainly, it takes a careful reading of the play to discover stakes, and it takes a strong and resourceful actor to play them. Imagine playing the role of one of the student card players in a scene where the bet was 25 cents. Now imagine playing it with the bet at $500.00. What different things would you be doing in these two scenes to show the different level of the stakes?

As you play higher stakes in a role (and in real life situations), you can easily notice some physical and emotional things about yourself that are, indeed, more dramatic and energized. Your heart may be pounding, your voice tense and hard, your hands damp and sweaty, your focus intense and narrow. You are engaged. On the other hand, the weak actor uses little of himself in performing; he uses little of his own energy; he plays the stakes so low, it is as though his character does not care at all what happens. Neither will his audience.

The strong actor, the one who plays the stakes as high as they are called for in the scene, has engaged her whole physical and emotional self into the role. She can tell she is in the moment, alive, dynamic, and connected to the action of the play; so can her audience.

Some Stakes Exercises

Work with a partner in one or more of the following situations. Rehearse and develop a scene that will last no more than a minute or so. In the improvisations where you develop dialogue, try to keep the dialogue nearly the same in each version. You are trying to change the stakes, not re-write the scene.

Highs and Lows   Rehearse several of the following activities, making certain to show the change in stakes in the different versions:

Try to open a jar:
1. as though you are bored and half asleep;
2. as though it will explode if you shake it or if you do not get it open in 15 seconds.

Call out for your friend in the next room:
1. as though you didn't care if he was there or not;
2. as though you were about to be eaten by a giant snake.

Talk to your mother on the phone about your OK grades:
1. as though you really wanted to watch TV instead;
2. as though you might get $50 from her for having brought up your GPA. (Change only the stakes, not the conversation.)

Sit in your chair and watch the people in the airport walk by you:
1. as though you have another 3 hours to wait for your plane;
2. as though the guy who is picking you up is somewhere in the crowd, wearing a green shirt, and you have never seen each other before.

Get the Door   You and your roommate are sitting on the couch watching TV. The doorbell rings, and neither of you want to get up to get it. You each want the other person to open the door. Play this first with low stakes. Repeat the scene (and dialogue) with high stakes.

What'a Ya Wanna Do?   You and a friend are sitting in the park, trying to decide how to spend the afternoon. Neither of you has much at stake at first, but as the scene goes on, each of you becomes more and more committed to what you want to do—not what the other wants.

Advocating and Commitment

If you are working on a role and you don't like the character, then you haven't done enough work on the role; you haven't found out what makes this character's intention so important to him or her. If you are working on a role and you find your mind wandering in the middle of a scene, then you haven't committed yourself to your character. If you are working on a role and it seems a lot like others you've played, then you haven't committed yourself to your craft; your tools or your observation of humanity are insufficient.

You may find that your character behaves in ways that are abhorrent or puzzling to you. You would never steal, or murder, or betray a friendship. But sometimes your character does, and if you are to do a committed job of portraying your character, you must get inside your character's skin. You must understand why the character does what he or she does. Figure out how your character justifies his or her behavior. (Hint: it usually has to do with the importance of the intention and how high the stakes are.) Remember, it is not your job to judge your character's behavior as you might be tempted to do in everyday life. Rather, your job is to present your character's actions as an advocate.

Commitment

So often in life we are put in the situation of needing to compromise. But isn't it exciting when we decide to vary this pattern and commit to something fully, regardless of the long-term consequences?

> What do you commit to in your life?
>> to getting an education?
>> to living life to its fullest?
>> to another person?
>> to God?

The actor's job is to give the audience that vicarious experience of living fully and dangerously in search of fulfilled intention. There is something life-affirming in this all-out risk, this rejection of the safe route, this need to assert one's own sense of what is right or just or necessary.

The audience doesn't pay to see an ordinary person go through minimally important events in his or her life. They pay to see a person who may be ordinary but who has a strong commitment to his or her goals (intention) go for it. They want to see what happens when this person comes up against obstacles and finds ways to get around them. They want to see this person give 100 percent to his or her intention. They want to see this person put everything toward that goal or die trying. That's what they want to do in their own lives, but usually can't.

Thus, as an actor, you must commit all of your mental, physical, and spiritual energy to your craft and to each individual role. You must commit to your craft in order to be able to portray the character to your full capacity. And you must commit to each role in order to advocate that character's quest.

CHAPTER THREE EXERCISES

1. Contrapuntal Argument:
    a. Set up simple circumstances (i.e., roommates or spouses in their home). Pick opposing intentions which directly involve the other person (i.e., make the other person admit it was their fault that the burglar was able to get in and steal everything).
    b. You have one minute. On "Go!" you must accomplish your intention with everything you have. Listen carefully to every bit of information that comes to you from your partner. But do not stop talking. (You will discover that you can listen and talk and think at the same time.) Two things you may not use: corporal attack and foul language or insults. On "Stop!" you must stop.
    c. Debrief and talk about partners and relationship, about emotion and intention.

2. Partner Intention/Obstacles

    Pick one of the following sets and work with a partner. Remember to achieve your intention through them.

    1. Get your partner to smile or laugh.
    2. Get your partner to calm down.

    1. Make your partner leave the room.
    2. Take possession of every bit of the space of this room.

    1. Take a nap.
    2. Tell your partner something very important about yourself.

3. This is an exercise to get you to interact truthfully with your partner. Sit facing each other. Each of you take one of the lines in the pairs of lines which follow:

    "I won't let you go."
    "You must."

    "You can't do this to me."
    " You don't understand, do you?"

    "Talk to me about all this."
    "I can't. Not now."

    Now sit facing your partner and explore the relationship which evolves as you say the lines to each other. Here are some other tips to get the most from this exercise:
    a. Don't say anything unless you **have** to. Silence is always preferable over unmotivated speech or action. Just sit and look at each other until something needs to be said.
    b. Say your line over and over again if you need to, until you feel that you have made contact with the other person in a truthful way.
    c. Vary the ways you try to get through to your partner. Watch your partner and pick up on any cues you receive from them (verbal, visual, emotional, etc.).

4. In rehearsals of your next scene, test how well you listen.
   a. Decide with your partner to make small changes in dialogue which will change the direction of the scene.
   b. Rehearse with a couple of surprise changes. Improvise your way back to the scene as written.
   c. Debrief afterwards. Discuss how the scene digressed or changed. How did each of you react to the new information or new obstacles?

Tactics

TACTICS ARE ACTIONS

By now you are probably making preparations for your first assigned, scripted performance from a play.[1] You should have a reasonably clear idea of who your character is, and you probably have already worked with your scene partner on this assignment. So now it is just a matter of memorizing the lines and you will be a star, right?

Ah, if only it were so easy! In fact, some of your most important decisions and discoveries about how to play the character are still ahead for you. Recall that characters are people who want to achieve specific intentions, but they find obstacles standing in their way. They must take specific steps, commit specific actions to overcome those obstacles and achieve their goals. The actions they take are called **tactics.**

These tactics are actually choices—conscious decisions to perform specific actions to achieve something. All of drama is made up of characters who keep trying different means to obtain their overall goal or intention, and the best performances are by actors who have elected to have their characters make strong dramatic choices.

Consider for the moment how this works in your own life. What about the tactics you use personally to achieve your own intentions? Let's suppose you want to graduate from college (intention), but your parents cannot afford to pay for all of your college expenses (obstacle), so you have to find tactics to achieve your goal. For example, here are some tactics you might try:

work for a couple of years to save money;
borrow money from a rich aunt;
work part-time while you are in college;
live on almost nothing and beg from friends;
rob a bank.

Of course none of the scenes you will perform this semester are going to cover a whole college education, so let's take a closer look at this example of your own life in college. Let us suppose that as part of your overall intention of graduating from college, this semester you have the intention of passing your acting class; moreover, in order to pass the class you want to do well on this first acting scene. Your obstacle is that you don't know much about what your character is like. To overcome that obstacle and achieve your intention of getting a good grade you might try to:

bribe the teacher with a $100 bill;
rehearse a lot and collaborate with your scene partner;
do a long and careful analysis of the scene;
hide in the back of the class every day and hope you are not called on to perform.

You will surely notice that all of the above choices are not equally good ones from an ethical/moral standpoint. You probably wouldn't choose some of them for your own personal tactics. In the same way, when you explore a character's possible tactics, you will come up with some that are less appropriate or useful than others. You will need to make choices that are appropriate to the character's own background and sense of ethics.

Nested Intentions

You might also have noticed from the examples above how the intentions for you in these college student examples are **nested.** That is to say, each more specific level of the example has a separate intention. In the examples there is an overall intention: to graduate from college. But each related part also has its own, separate intention. They are all related to the overall intention (to graduate from college); but each in its place is a separate intention. Consider:

> Your overall intention is to graduate from college;
> But connected to that is your intention to do well in Acting class;
> And connected to that is your intention to do well in your first Acting Scene;
> And connected to that is your intention to get along with your scene partner;
> And connected to that is your intention to memorize your lines right away.

Nested intentions are something like those little hollow wooden dolls from Russia: the gaily painted doll opens up to reveal another doll inside that one, which opens up to reveal another doll inside that one, which opens up to reveal. . . . , etc.

It is the same way in a play analysis. The character has an overall intention, but there are other subordinate intentions that come up throughout the play, different, but all connected to the overall intention. And as the scenes of the play unfold, the character keeps facing different intentions.

Do note, at every point in the action of a drama, the character plays each intention as it comes up and stays within the moment of that intention until it is either achieved or replaced by another. You do that in this class!

You want to graduate, so you want to do well in this class, so you want to do well with your scene. But, one day in class the teacher suddenly asks you to explain the main points in Chapter Four of this text. As you begin to answer, your focus, your energy, and all your attention is devoted to a new intention: "To show the teacher you have mastered Chapter Four." The original intention is still there and governs your choices, but the moment—this present intention—is where you are now.

It is simplistic to say a character has only one intention in a play. He or she has many, and the successful actor plays each intention his or her character encounters in the course of the play's action. Each of these intentions, if well-chosen, should help the character get closer to achieving his or her overall intention for the play.

More on Tactics

Let's return to tactics. So far we have been talking about making choices in your own life. The same process of possibilities and choices are within every play you will ever read or perform. Your task as an actor will be to find the possibilities and make strong, dramatic choices in your acting of the characters. To do this you need to use strong, active verbs for your tactics. Let us consider a few exercises.

1. **Physical Choices.** Work with a partner. Sit in chairs facing each other. One of you has the intention of staying in your chair and going nowhere. The other has the intention of getting both of you to leave the room.

Without physically hurting yourself or your partner, and without speaking any words or making any sounds, each of you should try to achieve your intention. Spend about one minute doing this exercise.

What were the things each of you did? The actions you performed were **tactics**—actions taken to achieve an intention.

Now you and your partner should reverse intentions and, following the same ground rules (no hurting each other, no talking, etc.), spend another minute with each of you trying to achieve your "new" intention. Be certain the person now trying to get both of you to leave the room doesn't merely duplicate what the other partner did in the first version.

What new tactics were used?

2. **Oral Choices.** Repeat the same exercise with each of you taking a turn with each intention. This time, however, neither of you may move out of your chair or commit any large physical actions. Instead, you are to use sounds—any variety of sounds you like—but do not use normal speech, such as words or sentences. Spend about one minute pursuing your intentions. Then reverse intentions, being certain not to copy what each other just did.

Remember, as each of you worked through this exercise you were choosing and playing tactics.

3. **Verbal Choices.** Now you are to do the exercise with actual, recognizable words and sentences. This time, however, you will need to practice a while, deciding what each of you is going to say. Rehearse, select, and develop this as a one minute scene. You should spend about 10 minutes working out what you are going to do.

Do not try to say exactly the same thing each time you run the scene; focus on achieving your intention more than on writing a classic one act play. Work to keep each of your intentions and tactics similar each time you do the exercise in rehearsal.

Once you are comfortable with this verbal version of the exercise, it might be appropriate for the class to act as an audience and watch each pair do their "scene" for the whole group.

TACTICS ARE DRAMATIC CHOICES

In doing these exercises and in watching other teams do their versions, you probably noticed a wide range of tactics being used. Perhaps in doing the oral exercise someone whimpered to get his way (achieve his intention) while someone else moaned, or cried, or hummed, or yelled. And as each actor selected tactics such as these and carried them out, you could see that some choices were more dramatic than others.

Probably the most successful of these scenes were those where the actors had made clear and strong choices of what to do to achieve their intentions. Often the weakest performance of scenes—whether they are improvised like these or written by a famous playwright—lack success because the actor lacked the willingness to make dramatic and interesting choices.

In very much this same way, your task this semester in working with actual plays and the dialogue provided by the playwrights will be to select and perform tactics which are dramatic, interesting, and lively choices.

Remember as you are examining your character's possibilities in any scene that you are investigating your character's potential and limits, not your own. It's very important to explore all possibilities when determining the tactics that a character may employ in surmounting an obstacle and practice those choices in rehearsal. Tactical choices often make the difference between a creative, alive performance and a hum-drum one.

Let's consider a scene from *Romeo and Juliet,* Act One, Scene 5 for a moment.

When Romeo first enters the Capulets' masked ball with his friend, Mercutio, his intention in the moment is to find Rosaline, the girl who broke up with him. But when he sees Juliet, he abandons all thoughts of Rosaline, and pours out his thoughts about being smitten with the lovely Juliet: "O, she doth teach the torches to burn bright! . . . Did my heart love till now?"

The lines to be said are provided by the playwright, William Shakespeare. As we discover later in the play, Romeo's major intention in the entire play becomes something like "I sincerely want to make Juliet love me as much as I love her, and be with her forever." But right now in this scene, he is in a new environment, and he is compelled to speak about his new feelings for Juliet. Thus, a good choice to describe his intention in this scene might be to say, "He wants to find a way to talk to Juliet and get to know her." (Notice that this fits well with his overall intention to convince Juliet to love him.)

What are some different dramatic choices an actor might make here in playing Romeo in this scene? Remember: his intention for the scene is "to talk to Juliet."

WEAK TACTIC CHOICES	STRONG TACTIC CHOICES
to talk quietly about Juliet	to impress Juliet
to talk softly to his friend Mercutio	to make her love him
to smile shyly at Juliet	to show off and compliment her
to be himself	to act charming, confident, and bold

Notice that both sets of choices are possible for Romeo, and technically, all of them are correct choices. Romeo could be the mild and soft-spoken, shy guy described in the first column. In fact, there are scenes later in the play where he acts somewhat like that. But it is also possible in this scene that Romeo is going to do everything he can to be bold and charm Juliet. He is not going to waste his big chance!

Which choice is more dramatic and interesting? Which is likely to be a more believable and alive character? You can always justify having your character sit around and whimper every line without trying any action beyond speaking a slow, dull monotone. But what audience wants that? What playwright writes dialogue to have it performed in a dull and boring way? Make your choices of tactics dramatic and alive.

Like intentions, discussed in Chapter Two, think about and write out your tactics as active and dramatic verbs. We don't call dialogue "drama" for nothing. Make it dramatic!

In the study and rehearsal of any scene, you need to discover, select, and choose tactics—the actions your character uses to remove obstacles and to achieve intentions. As a scene progresses, or—as in the case of Romeo's actions in Act I, Scene 5—the character keeps using new tactics. In fact, the list of tactics above do fit Romeo's goal. He starts out bold—he does get Juliet's attention and has soon found a way to speak to her, to charm her.

For practice, you might make a photocopy of that scene and mark it at each specific place where a new tactic starts—a new action taken to advance the intention or remove the obstacle.

All of the tactics you find for your character in a scene can be put together as momentary adjustments in the action of the character in order to get him closer to his intention. If you keep strong connections between your character's intention and all of the tactics he or she uses, and choose tactics that will help you get around the obstacles, you will create an insightful, creative, and consistent performance. If any of your character's tactics are not consistent with the behavior or personality of the character, it's time to go back and reevaluate the tactic, and maybe even the intention. The more directly you can involve the partner in your tactic, the more success you are likely to have in making the scene come to life.

MEMORIZING IS A NECESSARY TASK

It is a long standing joke in theatre, but one that comes true at every full-length play performance. After you have spent weeks, even months trying to get your character developed, shaped, perfected, and brought to life, after hundreds of hours of rehearsal and struggle to find how best to make your character dynamic, dramatic, and believable, you finally do a public performance. Backstage after the performance, you stand in a kind of nervous haze: you have done it! You have managed to create a real flesh and blood character out of mere lines from a printed text. Then some friend who saw the show, usually someone not much versed in theatre, comes up to you and all he says is, "Gee, how did you learn all those lines?"

Well, the reality is that many newcomers to theatre do marvel at the memorization process. But in truth, it is not really a serious problem for most actors—even most beginning actors. And a good thing, too, since the real work of most acting is discovering what to do with the character, not learning what to say.

Nonetheless, all the preparation in the world is useless if you don't know your lines. You let your partner down, you put the audience in an extremely embarrassing situation, and you look like a complete failure. If you don't know your lines, you can't act at all, no matter how much preparation you've done. All you can do is stand there and struggle to remember what comes next. All of your energy is taken up with your unlearned lines, so you have no concentration left for the acting.

Not memorizing lines, or memorizing them incompletely, is probably the most common reason why beginning actors fail. Luckily, there's an easy way around this awful and embarrassing problem. All it takes is some conscientious work spread out over time. You cannot memorize your lines the night before your scene is due and expect them to stick in your mind. You have to start well ahead of it and keep at it. In psychological terms, you have to over learn your lines. If you can make yourself put in the necessary time to learn your lines thoroughly and well in advance, you can sail through your scene and put all your energy into the acting, where it belongs.

For most of us, memorizing lines is hard. It takes time and concentrated work, and unfortunately there's no way around that unpleasant truth. There are a few people who pick up lines easily and retain them. We call these actors "quick-studies" and the rest of us envy their gift. For almost all of us, though, the process of memorization boils down to one thing: REPETITION.

Line repetition is a pretty unglamorous process, but it needs to happen thoroughly and it needs to happen right from the beginning of the rehearsal process. You can't really begin to act at all, or to develop your character, until you have your lines (or are "off book"). Most of the actual work of acting, of discovering and developing character only happens once you are confident of your lines. So the sooner you get started, the better.

Remember that you have to learn not only your own lines word-perfect, but your cues as well. Cues are the words that your partner says that trigger your lines. Usually your cues are the last few words of your partner's lines. What your partner says makes your character need to say something. In most scenes, your lines usually need to follow your partner's lines immediately, without huge pauses in between. If you memorize both your cues and your lines, your dialogue will sound like real people talking and responding to each other.

Line-Learning Techniques

There are many different ways to memorize lines. Here are some specific methods to try in your search for the best way to memorize lines. Most actors develop their own favorite method or combination of methods; what works for one person does not work at all for another. The important thing is that you find a way to learn your lines that works for you, and then practice it conscientiously, all through the rehearsal process. Don't leave memorization until the night before your scene. Besides being terribly unfair to your partner, this is a guaranteed recipe for disaster.

You will notice that each one is a variation on the theme of REPETITION.

Visual Learner—learning by reading: Read the lines out loud over and over again until you can anticipate what they are. Then go down the script with a card covering the lines just below where you are. Try to do the lines yourself before lifting the card to see what they really are. Gradually wean yourself away from peeking. (See Tips below.)

Kinetic Learner—learning by writing: Write out your whole script in longhand, both parts of the scene. Read this out loud several times. Then write out the script again, including only your cues (the last part of your partner's preceding line) and your own lines. Study this carefully. Then see if you can write out the whole scene in the cue and line format. Check for accuracy with your script and repeat until you know your lines. (See Tips below.)

Aural Learner—learning by hearing: Put both sets of lines on tape (preferably with your partner's voice and your own), being careful to avoid any inflection or interpretation. Just get the words down. Listen to this over and over again until you can anticipate what comes next. Then make another tape which has just your partner's lines and blank space where your lines fall. Try to do the scene with the tape, checking with your script to see how you are doing. Once you are sure you have the lines, toss the script away. (See Tips below.)

Movement Learner—learning by doing: This method works best when the director has blocked your scene (see next section) ahead of time or if you and your partner have blocked the scene early in the rehearsal process. Set up a rehearsal space for yourself, complete with chairs (or whatever you need) and walk your blocking as you read your lines out loud. If you do not have the luxury of this kind of open rehearsal space, do the same thing in your bedroom or living room. Repeat the process until you no longer have to look at your script for blocking or lines. (See Tips below.)

Any of the above methods, either alone or in combination, will ground you solidly in your lines and in your scene. The following method is not effective, and is guaranteed to make your scene partner frustrated and angry, and to embarrass you in front of the class when you stand up to perform.

Bozo Rehearsal Learner—not learning at all: This is the least effective method and is greatly disliked by most directors and acting partners. You wait until rehearsal to learn your lines, staying on book until everyone else is off. Your repetition factor consists entirely of the time spent in rehearsal; you spend no time at all on your lines outside of rehearsal. Your work is sloppy and late in developing; worst of all, you have no character relationships with anyone else in the play. You can't listen and feel frightened whenever you come into rehearsal. (This actor never pays attention to the following Tips.)

Tips for Learning Lines
1. Say your lines out loud in each of these methods. You can't merely reproduce the words; you have to *say* and *mean* and *do* them.
2. Add in the movement as soon as you have the blocking; this will help you link the sense of the word to the action and to the environment.
3. Don't paraphrase. Learn your lines exactly as the author has written them. If a line isn't comfortable to you, find a way to make it your own. Do not change the author's lines. Learn them as written, and learn them word for word.
4. Don't fall into inflection patterns too early on. Your director or scene partner may have input that will change what you thought the line meant, or how you need to respond. Setting inflections too soon often precludes any other interpretation of the line, and prevents the scene from growing and changing as you discover more things about it.
5. Remember that you are setting the ground work for your character's emergence through you. Do this process thoughtfully and conscientiously and you will be rewarded with many further discoveries.

ANALYSIS OPTIONS

1. Tactic Analysis. It may be useful for you at this point to focus your analysis on the tactics your character will use in this scene from the play.

   Make a photocopy of the scene you are to perform. On that copy indicate in order with numbers each spot where your character uses a new tactic. On a separate sheet of paper write out what each of those specific tactics is, using the same numbers you have on the photocopy to indicate exactly where each tactic started in the dialogue.

   Remember to make dramatic choices, to use action verbs, and to be very specific.

2. Character Analysis. It may be useful for you to do a complete analysis of all character elements we have covered so far in the course. The following form does just that.

   It is helpful for you to remember this: a lot of actor preparation is detective work. Find out who your character is. Read the play again, re-read the scene. Make clear and dramatic choices about who your character is and what your character does in the scene.

   Note that this analysis includes a new section, "Behavioral Analysis." Here is where you need to be especially dramatic in your choices. Be certain to use active verbs to describe your active character.

   Use the Character Analysis forms provided (or follow the format on your computer or word processor).

CHAPTER FOUR EXERCISES

Name: _____

Character you are playing: _____

Title of play: _____

Author of play: _____

A. Basic Analysis

1. Biographical (the present)
   Name:

   Sexual Life, Experience, Attitudes:

   Age, Maturity Level:

   Physical Appearance (Notable, distinguishing characteristics; choice/style of clothing):

   Education, Intellect, Thinking Abilities:

   Social and Economic Background, Status:

   Emotional Characteristics, Typical Mood:

   General Personality:

2. Given Circumstances (pre-existing and existing conditions that affect his or her behavior) Present Locale and Situation:

Earlier Experiences or Situations of Note:

Actions Immediately Preceding This Scene:

B. Behavior and Goals
Intention for the play:

Intention for the scene:

Obstacles:
Internal

External

Partners (other characters in the scene)(how help/how hurt for each partner)

Tactics (what the character does to achieve his or her intention)(active verbs)
Tactic #1

Tactic #2

Tactic #3

Tactic #4

Tactic #5

Chapter 5

Performance Critiques

THE ART OF THEATRE

Some of the most interesting and most rewarding activities students experience while enrolled in an acting class are not gained in the act of performing, though being an actor certainly is an exciting part of the class. However, the process of becoming skilled critics of performances may be something they come to enjoy as much as acting itself.

You probably did not give it much thought when you first enrolled in the class, but a lot of time in acting is devoted to critical analysis. Now that you are experiencing the joys and hard work of doing rehearsed, memorized selections in class, you are likely to have seen critics in action—you, your class-mates, and your teacher. In fact, if you think about it, you are going to spend much more class time in a given semester seeing and talking about performances than in doing them yourself. Consider this: if you are in a typical class with 20 students, each doing 3 performances during the semester, you would see 60 scenes performed, but you are only going to be a performer in 3 of them!

Even if you did nothing more than watch all those performances, you would develop a better understanding of what acting is, and how it can be effective or weak. But, if you really want to improve your own art as an actor, you need to work to expand your critical judgments about acting. You need to become a critic, for it is through the careful consideration of the work of others that you gain insights into what you yourself need to do to enhance your own work.

Most of the time acting students become pretty good critics of performance without much prompt-ing. Everything you see as performance outside of class will spark thoughts in your head about how well or poorly the "performer" is doing. Actors in plays that you see, TV shows and movies, even the performers in 30-second commercial breaks will all bring to your mind thoughts about how well they are playing their intentions, their obstacles, how believable and truthful they are—or are not.

But finally and most importantly, being a critical observer of acting is valid and important precisely because theatre, and specifically acting, is an art. It is about the expression of the human condition in ways that touch and move us. It is an art because it concerns itself always with how to try to achieve the truth of a performance, a character, or even an entire play.

It is not a finite science like basic math where the process is to find the one correct answer. Acting is a process of attempting ways to do something creative, not proving rights and wrongs. And as such, it is constantly open to discussion, evaluation, and reinterpretation. Why else would any of us ever go to see a play that we have seen done before? Why else would so many different actors all want to play some of the same characters whenever they can?

Great insights may come from being able to discuss a performance, to consider its daring, its hon-esty, its success, and to reflect on others' ways to do it.

THE SKILL OF BEING CRITICIZED

Good, experienced actors not only learn how to accept criticism but to appreciate and welcome it. As actors gain more experience, they generally crave criticism; it is a rare experienced actor who wants no feedback from others regarding the value, appropriateness, and usefulness of his or her acting choices. In truth, most play directors are swamped by actors who want to hear detailed feedback about every part of their performance.

So it is important that you learn to really hear any information that others will give you about your work. Remember that criticism does not only mean negative comments. A good place for you to start as the performer being criticized is with the realization that acting is an art form, and, as art, is naturally open to discussion and reflection. Look forward to finding out whether acting choices you made were strong or weak. For example, anticipate hearing about the impact those choices had on the audience and how they relate to the play. This is how an actor learns.

Some Specific Points to Focus On:

1. Realize there is no such thing as a perfect performance. No one, not even such greats as Lawrence Olivier or Katharine Hepburn, did performances that couldn't have been different, better executed, altered, or improved. This is an art form; we need to talk about many ways to do the acting, not the "one true way."
2. Recognize the distance between you and the character you play. Certainly that was you up there doing the scene, but we, the audience, are going to talk with you about what your character did, how the choices and actions of the character affected us. It is not a failing on your part to have come up with character actions we disagree with or have alternate opinions about. You are hearing useful information about audience reactions.
3. You are the target of critical observations only when you do half-hearted and poorly rehearsed work. Bring your best efforts to class and the commentary will always be useful.
4. Just listen to what the others have to say. This is not a time to argue, fight, become defensive, or make excuses. Take notes to refer to later. You just did your performance; now listen to what they have to say. A few pointers to help you with this:

   Sit next to your partner in front of the group;
   Write down everything everyone says;
   Don't defend your work at all;
   Just listen, and say thank you!

Taking critiques from your teacher and classmates is the only way to really tell whether you did what you intended to do or what you thought you were doing. Strive to find out how other people respond to your work.

Later, after the others have finished their comments, and you have achieved a little distance from what they said and what you had hoped they might have said, you can go over your notes, first with your partner, and then with your teacher (if you like) and figure out what was really said. Then you can adjust your scene in brush-up rehearsals so that you make both what the audience sees and what you have done more clear and effective during the final performance.

The whole purpose of doing your scene in the first place was to bring a specific character to life for your audience. During the critique session, you will be listening to find out what the audience actually got from the performances. It is helpful during that process to keep your own focus on the specific elements of the scene which you had been working to achieve in the first place.

Here is a list of specific points to focus on as the audience and teacher critique you:

1. Did the audience figure out what intention you were playing?
   Did they think you were playing a different intention?
   Did they think you should have been playing a different intention?
   Was your intention the strongest choice you could have made?

2. Did they understand the obstacles?
    Did they see what you were struggling against?
    Did they see the internal obstacles; the external obstacles?

3. Were the different sets of tactics clear?
    Were the transitions apparent between sets of tactics?
    Were the reasons for tactic changes clear and appropriate?
    Did you use enough tactics?
    Did you change your tactics as a response to what the other character did?

4. Did you and your partner create a clear and believable relationship?
    Were you strongly relating to each other?
    Was each of you attempting to affect the other's behavior?
    Did the audience care about what happened to the characters?

5. How did they respond to your individual character?
    Were your character's emotional reactions clear and appropriate?
    Were the physical actions you chose believable and pertinent?
    Did they care about your character? (Remember, it may be appropriate for them to hate or love your character. Any audience reaction is better than indifference.)

6. Was your energy high and directed at accomplishing your intention?
    Was your concentration strong?
    Did you externalize your attention by focusing on the action of the scene?
    Did you play the stakes high enough to affect the audience?

The responses you get to these issues are really at the heart of acting; they tell you what the audience actually got. So, what you thought you were doing, or what you intended to do, isn't what matters to the audience. It's what the audience understood you to be doing, and what they felt about your performance, that is the key to how your scene went. As you continue to rehearse and work your scene later, you can adjust your performance to narrow the gap between what they actually saw and felt, and the reaction that you wanted.

THE SKILL OF THE CRITIC

Beginning actors often try to reject their duty as critics of performance. They will say either they don't know enough to be critics, or they don't know enough about the scene being done to say anything useful. Or they feel that it is not fair to say anything "bad" about someone else's performance.

In fact, nothing could be less fair in an art form like acting than to say nothing about each other's work. This is a skills class, a process class with one of its chief purposes being the job of training the actor to convey things to the audience. Without responses back from the audience, the actor would be performing in a vacuum.

The concern about "not knowing anything about the play" is really without much merit. Have you ever seen a movie or a TV show for the first time and found things in it that were effective and, likewise, things that made it unbelievable? Were you able to do that only when you knew about the movie in the first place and had seen it before? Of course not. We are skilled social beings, and whenever we are in any social situation—even as audience members of a live performance—we are constantly taking notice of what is happening as well as making judgments about what we are seeing.

Even though you may tell your teacher "I don't know enough about this to say anything," you actually know a lot if you were simply paying attention. All you need to do is decide if it was believable or not, and exactly why. Probably, if you are honest with yourself, you form opinions about every scene you see in class, while you see it. But you may still have a hard time talking about it.

Let's look at ways to make criticism easier and more clear.

As you reflect on the comments you get from your scene work, or that you make as a critic of other scenes, realize that here are two important, quite different things to gain in the criticism of performance work. One is the feedback of what was done: Could the audience see what the actors were trying? Did it get across? Were the actor's energy, commitment, intensity, and stakes clear enough? Was there clear and purposeful movement? Were the lines audible, rehearsed, and appropriately loud? This kind of critique is called descriptive criticism.

Descriptive criticism describes, it mirrors, what the performers did. It is not a judgment or value process, but merely a reporting on what the viewer saw. This kind of criticism can be particularly helpful in defining what actually happened in a performance. It avoids a lot of potential argument in a critique session and stays with the observable facts.

Descriptive criticism is often a good place for novice critics to start. It provides information about what the audience got from the scene. It merely includes a discussion and description of what you saw, the actual physical description of what went on. As a hypothetical example, it could include such statements as: I saw the two actors sit in their chairs during the entire scene. I saw that John was very quiet and soft spoken throughout most of the scene. I did not see him change mood, energy, or vocal level during the scene. I saw that Julie, the other actor in the scene, started out very quiet but became much louder and faster as the scene went on. She had three or four different actions in the scene.

Descriptive criticism describes what you saw. It focuses on *what* was done in the scene.

Evaluative criticism, on the other hand, is judgment and includes making value decisions. In addition to describing a performance, it includes judgments about the appropriateness of things in the scene. It is comparative, balancing what was done against what ought or might have been done in the performance. It focuses on how a scene performance might be made clearer or stronger. A hypothetical example of a performance critique could include such statements as: I saw the two actors sit in their chairs during the entire scene, and if they had moved around each other it would have been more believable, because the scene seemed to be about two people trying to physically dominate each other. I saw John use only the tactic of being quiet and soft spoken, but I think he needed to try tactics using more energy and force, because the lines in the scene describe him as shouting and blowing up.

Evaluative criticism evaluates, it judges. It focuses on *what could have been done* in the scene to make it more effective for the audience.

Evaluative criticism is a bit harder for some beginning actors to do, both because it forces you to think about what was done and how it should be done at the same time, and because it is where the critical statements get more pointed. "I saw that you sat in the chair the whole scene" is a pretty safe, descriptive comment to make to your fellow students. There is little potential friction in that statement. But it is harder to state an evaluative comment, one that shows a judgment: "I believe it would have been a stronger, more effective choice to get up and move around during the big fight scene."

Remember that evaluative criticism is important. The art of theatre is found there, in the endless considerations and attempts at doing characters and scenes in different, interesting ways, in the trying to make the drama more clear, more believable, more truthful about the human condition.

THE ART OF THE CRITIC

Good criticism involves looking at performances with an eye to actually examining the choices the actors have made. That is, you consciously reflect on what they are doing and what they might have or ought to have done instead of or besides what they actually did. It is not always easy to do these two things at the same time.

Contrasting the Actual with the Possible

This requires a thought process that you often use in many situations, but may not have yet been much aware of in viewing performances. You may think that the way a play is performed is the only way it can be performed, that what you see is the only way to do it, that the characters have a life separate from the actors who play them, and that what you see onstage at any particular performance is therefore "right."

But let's consider real life for a moment. You go to a party. You meet someone you have never seen before. That person starts talking to you about some topic you have not heard much about. Just as soon as this conversation starts, you are making judgments and critical observations about the conversation and about the person himself.

You may decide of this person at the party, "This guy is a real yawn." Or, "This guy is a lot of fun." Or even, "This guy is really weird." You reach your critical decision because even as he spoke, you were comparing what he was doing with what he might have done. For example, let's do the "drip" version. Here, this guy is dominating the conversation with some topic you could care less about. He might at least have asked you something about yourself. At least he should notice that you are looking around for a chance to get away from him, and he ought to have ended his boring monologue and let you move on.

You reach all those judgments quite fast. And you got to all of them by contrasting in your mind what he was doing with what he could have or ought to have done. What you are doing—what all of us social beings do all the time—is constantly run a process in your mind that evaluates what the person is doing, and what they might do to be better or more effective. We do exactly the same thing in actor critiques. You compare the actual with the possible.

Go back to the hypothetical scene used to illustrate descriptive and evaluative criticism, between John and Julie. As John sits in his chair the entire scene, you see that he could be standing up and moving around. Especially as his lines start to be about controlling and dominating her, you see the difference between him sitting quietly and the lines being about someone who is physically aggressive. You see an actor who made weak tactic choices (sit in the chair and talk softly) and you also envision the much stronger tactic the lines seem to define (to get up and intimidate her with your presence).

You compare the actual with the possible. You do it in life all the time. Start to do it while observing performances and in critiquing them.

Look for the Evidence

Being a critic of acting requires you to be a good detective. In much the same way you need to do detective work in figuring out your own character in preparing a scene for performance, so you have to examine the evidence in critiquing the work of other actors. But again, it is not exact and precise, like solving a math problem. It is imaginative and comparative.

What is it you compare in a performance? Well, you know by now that you are looking at the same things in performances that you strive for in your own character work: intention, obstacles, tactics, and stakes. And you find this, both in your acting and in watching other performances, by comparing what is done with the source—the text of the play.

What the character does and what the character ought to do, the actual and the possible, come from an analysis of the text; that is, from the actual dialogue and action of the play. The two classic places where you find out what is going on:

What the Characters Say. The dialogue, both from the character and from other people in the play as they talk about this character, is very important. Often very obvious clues are written into the dialogue. "Don't raise your voice to me." "Please don't cry anymore." "Will you hurry up and drink your coffee?" "Please sit down." All of these represent just a few of the thousands of information lines that are in dialogue which tell us, the audience, what is or what ought to be taking place on stage. Frequently, characters will spend a lot of time talking about someone who is not yet in the scene. They usually have very useful evidence about what the character is supposed to be like. Likewise, when a character leaves the scene, the remaining people usually say things which give us more evidence.

What the Characters Do. The action of the play is a very useful source of understanding about what could be possible (or probable) for a character. The degree to which a character is motivated, the extent to which they will go—the level of the stakes for them in the play—come from looking at the overall action. Especially the ending action for a character will tell us a lot. Does the character kill himself or herself (or someone else)? Does the character end up getting what he or she wanted? Does he or she have a big change of heart, or of idea, or of purpose by the end? How large, heroic, brave, and noble (or how cowardly, inept, weak, and dishonest) are the things the character does?

But your mental process of comparing actual and possible character (and actor) choices also requires some creative thinking on your part. You already have the experience to do it automatically with the way people in our culture dress. You keep an almost unconscious balance running of what you consider "acceptable dress" and what you see people wear. If a guy comes into Chemistry class on a December morning wearing a swimsuit, you need only a thousandth of a second to decide that is an inappropriate clothing choice.

With acting it takes a bit more practice. Keep practicing. As soon as the performer enters the stage, ask yourself: Is that action appropriate? Is that choice clear? Is that movement useful? What do their actions communicate to you? Keep thinking what they might have done as you see what they actually do. Keep reflecting on how much the lines of the play describe and justify the character you see being performed.

Judging acting is a bit like judging the clothes people wear. Look at what your fellow students have on in class. There are no hard and fast rules about what is right or correct. People are probably wearing all kinds of looks: preppy, jock, nerd, grunge, dork, and cool are just a few "looks" that are current and accepted. In a sense there is no "right way" to dress for class. But whatever choices people make in clothing and style communicates something very specific about them to the rest of the world.

In much the same manner, the way a role is performed is not usually described as precisely "right" or "wrong." There are a wide range of interpretations that are possible, and only a few will be so extreme as to be considered wrong. It is hoped that by this point in the course you have seen what happens onstage is the result of choices made by the actors, based on what is given in the script. Some choices—the strongest, clearest, and most emotionally engaging ones—are better choices than weak, confusing, or disengaged ones.

As an educated observer of acting, you must look at others' work in terms of how they have applied the basic acting principles, and how well their choices work to create a physical and emotional reality onstage, with characters that you believe in and care for, and who communicate personality and situations clearly. Always try to be certain their choices are justified by the action and dialogue of the play as being actual and possible.

PERFORMANCE CRITIQUE OPTIONS

Do one of the following critique options on the performance of a full-length stage production. While the two options are different in their details, several instructions apply to either:

a. You are to write a critique of only one of the actors in the production you see. It is not necessary that you know as soon as the play starts who you are going to cover, but as the production moves along, be certain to have selected someone who is one of the main characters in the play.

b. Do not take notes during the show. Make notes at intermission, or immediately afterwards if you need to. It's rude to the actors onstage and very distracting to other members of the audience for you to sit there busily playing out your role of dutiful critic, writing furiously and self importantly during the performance.

c. Do not answer items in your paper about the character merely by reporting what the actor did. Focus on what the play calls for in the character, not just what the actor did in the performance. This is a critical analysis, not a book report.

d. Submit your finished paper by the second class after you see the performance—typed, double-spaced, and 3–5 pages long.

Option One: General Performance Critique

Provide clear and specific answers for each of the following items. Be certain to cover those points within each item which are most notable or most important for this character in this play.

The Name of the Play, When, and Where You Saw It

The Name of the Character and the Name of the Actor

Item 1: **Character Personality**

Provide a discussion of the character's overall personality, including such information as physical, emotional, intellectual, and ethical characteristics.

Item 2: **Character Background**

Provide a discussion of the character's specific background, including such details as education, training, social and economic status, and home life.

Item 3: **Character Behavior**

Identify and discuss the 4 or 5 most notable tactics the character commits in the course of the play. Identify the character's main intention in the whole play. Explain how those 4 or 5 tactics succeed (or fail) for the character in achieving that main intention.

Item 4: **Actor Choices**

Discuss several notable and specific things the actor did to make the character come to life as an appropriate, believable, and dramatic creation.

Discuss several notable and specific things the actor either failed to do or did poorly in attempting to bring the character to life. (These are things that were clearly called for in the script or in the action of the play but which the actor failed to achieve.)

Option Two: Detailed Character Analysis Critique

The following acting critique is the format for your responses once you have seen the production, chosen the character you wish to critique, and are ready to begin writing. Either use the pages that follow or follow the format with your computer or word processor.

The Name of the Play, When and Where You Saw It

The Name of the Character and the Name of the Actor

(Keep sections 1, 2, and 3 brief and to the point; the major portion of this analysis is part 4.)

1. **Biographical** (the present)

   Sexual Life, Experience, Attitudes

   Age, Maturity Level

   Physical Appearance (notable and distinguishing characteristics)

   Education, Intellect, Thinking Abilities

   Social and Economic Background, Status

   Emotional Characteristics, Typical Mood

   General Personality

2. **Given Circumstances** (pre-existing and existing conditions that affect his or her behavior)

   The Present Locale and Situation

   Earlier Experiences, Situations of Note

   Action Immediately Preceding This Scene

3. **Behavior and Goals**

   Overall Intention for the Entire Play

   Obstacles:

   Internal

   External

4. **Critique of Actor's Performance**

   Discuss your reaction to the actor's performance, based on the elements you have identified and discussed above. Give examples to support your contentions. This is the bulk of your critique.

   1. Did the actor present a believable character and an interesting performance? Did you care about what the character did and how he felt?

   2. Did the actor create believable relationships?

   3. Could you see the intentions, obstacles, and tactics? Did they seem appropriate to you? Were they the strongest possible choices?

4. What worked well? Were there any "special moments" in the play in which your character participated?

5. Which moments in which your character participated did not work so well? Why not?

6. What would you have done differently if you were playing the role?

Chapter 6

Rehearsal and Theatre Ethics

THE IMPORTANCE OF REHEARSING

The word "rehearse" comes from an old French word that means "re-harrow." A harrow is an agricultural implement that looks like a huge comb with long, curved teeth. Every time a farmer drags a harrow over a field, new things turn up. Sometimes they're bones or old tree roots. But sometimes the farmer finds buried treasure when dragging the harrow again through the field. That's what happens in a good rehearsal period, too. You start out with a pretty simple approach to your scene, and every time you go over it, either alone or with your partner, you come up with new ideas and deeper understandings of your scene, your character, and your acting choices.

The rehearsal period is when you and your partner figure out what the scene is about and how it's put together. Then you decide on how to perform your scene so that the audience understands it. Rehearsals can be exciting, because if you do your work thoroughly, in addition to finding major new understandings in your scene and character, you'll end up with a well-prepared scene.

On the other hand, the surest way to blow a scene or monologue is to skimp on actor homework and rehearsals. Under-rehearsing is the single biggest reason that student actors get into trouble with their performances. It's very obvious when watching a scene whether the actors have rehearsed enough to really understand the scene and be able to perform it. There is no substitute for thorough homework and active rehearsal. You will foul up badly if you neglect this.

Remember: the point of performing a scene is not simply to show the audience that you have memorized your lines and can show off emotions. The idea of performance is to bring the character to full and vivid life before the audience, with all the reactions, changes, thinking, and discoveries that character actually has. The rehearsal process is the only way for you to find the living elements and depth which will truly bring the character to life in the scene. It is in rehearsal that you discover, learn, and become comfortable being the character.

A PLAN FOR REHEARSING YOUR SCENE

It's impossible to do all the necessary rehearsal the night before your scene is due. Generally, figure on 1 to 1-1/2 hours of rehearsal per minute of stage time, not counting homework time. So a 4-minute scene needs 4 to 6 hours of rehearsals, spread out over several days. Rehearsing needs to be spread out over time because the creative process doesn't work well unless there's time to think and internalize what you've done in between active rehearsals.

This rehearsal plan will give you plenty of time to develop your scene into something interesting and to rehearse it thoroughly.

Rehearsal 1 (1 hour)

1. Meet with your partner and go over your scene.
2. Start to get very specific.
   a. Talk a bit about the characters each of you will play.
   b. Make some notes about your character. Pay particular attention to establishing your character's intention. Be as specific as you can, but expect to modify your initial choices as you rehearse.
   c. Establish the given circumstances for the scene. Discuss the relationship which exists between the characters of the scene.
   d. Identify the obstacles each of your characters face.
   e. Then go over the sequence of tactics that your character uses to overcome each obstacle in the scene and make them as clear as you can. (Remember, you may need to use several tactics for one obstacle. Tactics are not always successful. If one does not work, you will *change* your tactic and try another.)
      - Be sure that each tactic one character uses causes some response from the other character.
      - Be sure that your character changes tactics when he realizes that the current tactic isn't working.
      - Be sure that each successive tactic is in some way an escalation of the situation (thus building tension) and of your character's attempt to realize the intention.
      - Allow the frustration of failure or the joy of success affect your character's subsequent behavior.
3. Read the scene aloud together, keeping the given circumstances, your intention, and its associated tactics firmly in mind but without getting too intense about anything yet.
4. Discuss what happened. Adjust any intentions, tactics, or relationships that aren't clear. Clarify the obstacles. Throughout rehearsals you will continue to try things and adjust them until you get your scene as strong as possible.
5. Read the scene aloud together again; this time make your character try as hard as possible to achieve the intention.
6. Discuss what happened. Make some notes for yourself.
7. It is important to remember here that rehearsal is not just for memorizing your lines, nor is just running your lines enough to perform a successful scene.
8. Remember, this is a *collaborative* process. NEVER try to direct your scene partner! Stay focused on what *your* character is trying to get or accomplish. ALWAYS respect your acting partner and their character choices.
9. Set a time for your next rehearsal.

Before Rehearsal 2 (1/2 hour)

1. Go over your lines. Lines should be memorized with their associated tactics by now. As you rehearse, visualize the other character and what he does to prevent your character from achieving his intention. Think of new tactics that you might try.
2. Think about your character. Try to visualize how he looks, dresses, and moves. Think about your character's favorite books, shows, and music. What kind of childhood did he have?
3. Go over your given circumstances. Make sure that they always enhance your acting. Think about your "as ifs."
4. Make notes.

Rehearsal 2 (1 hour)

1. Share with your partner the things you have figured out between rehearsals.
2. Run your scene. Put in all the things you know about your character. Play your intention strongly. Change tactics clearly. Try to affect the other character as much as possible. Keep the stakes high.
3. Talk about what happened. Did your chosen actions and tactics create a clear cause-and-effect path through the scene? Make any appropriate adjustments.
4. Run the scene again. Make sure that your character's thoughts are strongly focused in the scene. The thoughts should center on how much your character wants his intention, and what he needs to do to get it, also, how he feels about the other character and about what is going on between them.
5. Talk about what happened. What new information did you discover about your character's thoughts, feelings, and behavior? Make any appropriate adjustments.
6. Run the scene again. This time, trade characters (you may use the script if necessary). Using what you know from your rehearsals, try to gain the other character's intention. Allow the other character to affect yours.
7. Talk about what happened, and make adjustments if necessary.
8. Run the scene one last time. Play your assigned character, and make the scene as life-like as possible. Try to achieve your intentions by using your tactics as strongly, and yet subtly, as possible. Allow what is going on in the scene to affect your character's behavior, thoughts, and emotions.
9. Talk about it. Make notes about the new things you have discovered, and the old things that still work.
10. Set a time to meet again.

Before Rehearsal 3 (1/2 hour)

1. Go over your lines several times a day. As you run lines, think of your intentions, obstacles, tactics, given circumstances, and relationship to the partner.
2. Think about your character a lot. When you get new insights or ideas about your character or the scene, write them down.

Rehearsal 3 (1 hour)

1. Share with your partner your new thoughts.
2. Run your scene 3 or 4 times. Try to affect the other character strongly. As you make new discoveries, allow them to become an integral part of your acting. Look for the places where things seem to escalate or change.
3. Talk about what you've done after each run through.
4. Make some notes.
5. (Optional exercise) Go out for coffee in character. React to things as your character would. Have a few laughs. Be sure to make notes.

The Preview of Your Scene

1. Before the preview of your scene, go over your lines and actions several times a day. Think about your character a lot.
2. THEN GET UP THERE AND DO YOUR BEST.
3. After your preview, take notes on the responses from your teacher and classmates. Schedule a brush-up rehearsal with your partner.

Before the Brush-up (1/2 hour)

1. Go over your notes and the teacher's response. Decide what you can do to adjust the scene to make it work better.
2. Go over your lines several times a day.

Brush-up Rehearsal (1 hour)

1. Talk about your preview as well as the notes and comments you got in class. Discuss the specific points of strength and of weakness in your scene that were identified. Share any ideas about how to improve the scene.
2. Work through the scene, step by step; stop at each weak point. Go over and try to discover alternate ways to perform those specific weak points noted in class as needing adjustment.
3. After you have experimented with ways to overcome the weak points and sections, do a run-through of the scene. Strive with your partner to make each moment work clearly for both of you in terms of intention, obstacles, and tactics. Keep the stakes high.
4. Pick the most appropriate and dramatic tactics you can find. Don't stick with old choices if you can find better ones.
5. Run the scene two more times, trying to polish and set the new changes you have put into the scene. Don't add more now; perfect what you have.

The Performance (5 minutes)

1. Before the performance, take a few minutes with your partner to go over your lines and your notes, to remind yourselves of everything you know about your characters. Breathe deeply. Concentrate on getting your character's intention.
2. THEN REALLY COMMIT TO YOUR INTENTION IN PERFORMANCE.

Congratulations! You have completed the entire process of preparation and performance of a scene. It's a long and demanding process. But the rewards (and the training) are worth the effort. Theatre training reflects the kind of discipline necessary in athletics or the military. Serious theatre directors will hire actors who have the traits that come from focus and hard work: outgoing, team players, good problem-solvers, conscious of the efforts of others, able to adjust to a variety of situations and needs. Actors must be extremely dedicated to their craft in order to accomplish career goals.

MUSCLE MEMORY: ACTING AS A SKILL

Much of the exploration about who characters are and what choices they make comes only during rehearsal. It is where important discoveries are made by the actors. However, besides all the intellectual work which happens in the rehearsal process, there is quite a different process at work which, in the end, is no less important than the intellectual understanding of the scene. It is **muscle memory.** Muscle memory is a term most closely related to sports. It is the process of training the body (both its emotional and physical components) to perform repetitious functions automatically, or at least nearly automatically.

Consider sports; for example, baseball. The beginner at baseball has a lot to learn about how to hit a ball; which hand to place where on the bat, how to change his stance, which way and how much to turn the shoulders, how to follow through a swing, where to look—the list can go on and on. The odds are high that when the beginner first steps up to bat that he will hear the umpire yell "Strike!".

Clearly, a successful batter—even on a little league—has to spend a lot of time at practice before being able to hit the ball accurately. If the batter wants to do well in actual games against a really experienced pitcher, there will need to be hours and days of batting practice.

Now, for a good baseball player or, for that matter, golfer, swimmer, fencer, or tennis player, or any person who uses their body in performance—for all these people—muscle memory is a very important function of their success. They have practiced certain moves so often and so well that they are automatic. Sure, the batter has to assess the pitcher, the pitch, and the best strategy for that moment in the game before he actually takes a swing. But long and careful practices have trained his body to act in the way he needs it to, without having to give any thought of how to go through the motions.

In exactly the same way actors train their bodies and their emotions to be there when they need them. You can easily see that sports demand skills which require physical and mental training. So does acting.

For the athlete, muscle memory is the trained ability of the body to perform functions with great precision, almost automatically. A good batter does not even have to think about turning the wrists out, widening his stance, and swinging out, wide, and ahead of the pitch. His training has prepared his body to react correctly. He will focus on making the decision to try for a line drive over third, and then his body will automatically take over.

The same is true for the rehearsed actor. She has rehearsed the scene a dozen times, has broken down each moment and change in tactics, and when the big discovery comes at the end of the scene, she doesn't even have to think about standing up, running across the stage to grab a weapon and defend herself. She is in the emotional and intellectual moment—she is focused and her body—because of rehearsal—has acquired the muscle memory to carry out the action that she has discovered and mastered in rehearsal. She is too busy living the life of the character she has perfected to have to stop and think about what she is supposed to do next.

Certainly you gain a lot of intellectual understanding of your character in rehearsal, but you are also developing the muscle memory to play the scene. The skills of how you speak, breathe, gesture, move—even the emotions you feel while doing these physical actions all become part of your body's memory systems. And when you act a well-rehearsed scene before an audience, those mastered skills are reflected in your performance. Rehearsal enables you to learn the scene; muscle memory allows you to live it.

OTHER IDEAS FOR GETTING TO KNOW YOUR CHARACTER

Many times when we tell a story about a friend, we imitate how they acted in a certain situation. The better you know the friend and the situation, the better your story will be. You need to know your character well, too. One good way to learn things about your character is to think about how he would react to various public situations and environments. How would she behave in a grocery store line, a movie theatre lobby, a polling place during an election, a jury-duty hearing? *Why?* What is it about your character's beliefs, traits, background, and needs that would cause them to react in a certain way?

Aside from all this rehearsal work, learning your lines, and figuring out who's getting what from whom, it's crucially important to get to know things about your character beyond what you've written in your Character Analysis sheet. Here are three examples of how to do that. These techniques can give you important insights into your character that you won't get in rehearsal. Thus they can enrich your performance, because the better you know your character the better you can act him or her.

The Line Rehearsal
1. Sit facing your partner and go over your lines until you are both word-perfect. Play your intentions and change tactics throughout this rehearsal, but concentrate mostly on learning your lines. Only then can you actually begin to rehearse the acting part of your scene.
2. Learn the other character's lines too, or at least your cues. Cues are what the other character says that makes your character answer. If you don't learn what prompts your character to speak

the next line, what *causes* your character to react, you've done only half your memorization work.

Note: Learn the character's train of thought as well as the literal words he or she uses. (See Chapter 7: Inner Life.)

The Knee-to-Knee Rehearsal (for Relationship and Truth)

1. Read the scene together out loud. Sit facing each other, so that your knees are almost touching. Here are the rules for this first reading:
   a. DON'T ACT. That is, don't put meaning or inflection into your voice, and don't move around. The scene will sound flat, but that's what you want at this point, because you're still trying to figure out what's going on in the scene.
   b. Never say a line unless you are looking at your partner and your partner is looking at you.
   c. Use this technique:

       Look down at your script.

       Grab only as many words with your eyes as you can comfortably remember. If you can only remember two or three words at a time, that's okay. Remember, this is a rehearsal technique; you use it only in rehearsal, never in performance.

       Look at your partner and make sure your partner is looking at you.

       Say as many words as you have grabbed. When you run out of words, look down at your script again and repeat the sequence of grabbing a few words, looking directly at your partner, and saying the words.

2. After you've gone through the script this way, stop and talk with your partner about what you found in the script. Questions to ask:

   Could we tell where the characters seemed to change thought or subject or intensity?

   Were there places where the characters seemed to need to do something?

   What action did they want to do?

   Which of your tactics seemed to work and which didn't? Don't be afraid to try new tactics during each rehearsal.

   Did you make the transitions between sets of tactics?

   What did the other character do that made your character need to change tactics?

The Grand Opera Rehearsal

1. Run your scene once at normal performance level. Do everything you have rehearsed and thought about. Really try to accomplish your intention.
2. Run your scene again. Play it as if you were in the Grand Opera. Do everything at the top of your voice, with huge amounts of energy. Run around the set and exaggerate your intentions and reactions. Fall to the floor and sob. Make huge extravagant gestures. Be "over-the-top." Have fun with the scene. Don't be afraid of being melodramatic. If you have to stop because you are laughing, that's okay. But try to get through the whole scene and make everything as big and loud as possible.

3. Run your scene twice more without stopping; try to retain the commitment and energy level of your huge rehearsal, but keep the scene within normal performance bounds. Make everything as clean and precise as possible. Concentrate on affecting your partner and accomplishing your intention. Pay close attention to the character's need to change tactics, and make those changes clearly. Work to accomplish your intention. Keep the stakes high.

Job Interview in Character

1. Ahead of time, decide what job your character is applying for, what experience you have had that is relevant, what particular time this is, and specifically where you are.
2. The class and instructor arrange themselves in a wide circle around the chair in which your character will sit.
3. When you arrive, the leader of the interview (instructor or other student) will ask you your name, address, and what job you are applying for. You will respond in character, setting up the rest of the improvisation with the information you have supplied.
4. The interview proceeds along traditional interview format, with members of the interview team asking appropriate questions. (Note: there is a responsibility on the part of the interviewers to help the actor by asking leading questions, not confusing ones.)
5. After several questions have been asked and answered (about 3 minutes), the leader will say, "Thank you, Mr./Ms. _____ for coming in today. We will be in touch." At this point, you leave in character and return as yourself, ready to take a spot on the interviewing team for the next character.

After class, make notes on what happened in this hypothetical interview. Consider the following types of questions:

How did my character feel when placed on the spot like this?

Did I/my character have enough confidence in my experience and abilities to present myself well?

Did I lie? Did I want to?

Did anything happen that left me at a loss?

Do I think I got the job?

Everybody in the Bus Station

1. This is a group improvisation. Set up the classroom to represent a bus station. Know where the vending machines are, where the notice board is, where the restrooms are, where the clock is, where the arrival doors are, and anything else that will make the circumstances believable. Agree on what time it is, and what the weather is. Each student portrays the character he or she is playing in his or her final scene.
2. Decide individually what has just happened to your character, where he or she is going, and why. Use information from the script of your play. Know where in the play your character is during this improvisation. (For example: has the storm happened yet?)

Taking Your Character for a Walk

Another good way to get to know your character is to go for a walk or for coffee with your scene partner, staying in character the whole time. Walking across campus together is a good way to find out how your and your scene partner's characters see the world outside of your scene. (Don't do anything foolish or dangerous, or anything that will get you into trouble. Respect others.) After this exercise, sit down and make notes on what your character did and how he or she reacted and felt about the experience. What did you learn about your character that you can apply to your scene?

Observation Exercise

See if you can spot someone on campus or in town who is like your character. Watch him or her carefully but unobtrusively for mannerisms, speech patterns, reactions, etc. Some of what you see may be helpful to you.

A REHEARSAL JOURNAL

An actor needs to take some notes that will allow him or her to plan and keep track of the rehearsal. If you go into each rehearsal knowing exactly what you want to accomplish, you will accomplish that and more. Planning your rehearsal goals will also help you and your partner focus on the work at hand, thereby avoiding critical or personal commentary on each others' work. Remember: an important rule here is never to attempt to direct the other actor. Explore YOUR character in relation to the other character, and the choices and reactions that work for your character. Do not try to second-guess or judge your scene partner. Let them explore their own character. A disciplined rehearsal frees you both for optimum creativity.

Every time you start an acting project, buy a notebook or loose-leaf binder and designate that it will be used for rehearsal notes. After each rehearsal, sit down with your scene partner and make some notes:

> review what you have accomplished
> old stuff which is getting better
> new stuff which worked
> old stuff which doesn't work anymore
> new stuff which didn't work, but gave you new ideas
> plan what you wish to accomplish next time

Then sit down by yourself and go over the same process. Think about what happened in the rehearsal and where you want to take this character. Always check your ideas with the text to see if you can support them.

REHEARSAL ETHICS

In the theatre there is a code of behavior, an etiquette. There are rules that everyone observes, just as in any sport or profession. You are cast for your scene or part in a production; you report for work; you get started on rehearsals. Your director or teacher fills you in on your responsibilities. But it goes beyond that. There are some basic rules which you need to know if you want to fit into the rehearsal/performance environment.

Do's

1. Do be on time for all rehearsals and performance calls. (No last-minute canceling, unless you are in an emergency room!)
2. Do be considerate to your fellow actors in every way you can. Consider the feelings and needs of the acting partner as well as your own as you rehearse.
3. Know your lines as soon as possible so you won't waste other's time, and you can REALLY get to work.
4. Bathe regularly and keep up with your other personal hygiene as well. Breath mints are a *must* if you have a kissing scene, or are close to another actor's face.
5. Do commit to making each other and the production as a whole look as good as possible. Everyone has the same goal: the best show possible!
6. Do develop a strong work ethic. You will get known in the theatre community as a reliable actor . . . or as an unreliable one. You choose.
7. Observe the Golden Rule of acting: Say nothing to another actor that you would not like said to you.

Don't's

8. Don't assume you can tease fellow actors about their performance unless you have already developed a level of trust which allows such joking.
9. Don't assume that because of the demands of the script, it's okay to touch a fellow actor in an aggressive or sexual way. Fights and sexy scenes need to be blocked out carefully with the physical and emotional safety of everyone kept in mind. Work with your director or teacher on this.
10. Don't goof off in rehearsal. You will get a bad reputation that may prevent you from getting cast again. Rehearsal is your job, develop a professional attitude—fast.
11. Don't take over a scene if you think that you are the one who has more experience in theatre.
12. Don't let the other actor do so either. It's a partnership whenever you rehearse. Generally, the reverse is true: the *most* experienced actors are very generous in rehearsal, and will go out of their way to collaborate.
13. Don't bring your own personal baggage into the rehearsal or production environment. You are not there to be the center of attention, or to be taken care of; you are there to contribute to the good of the show. Don't be a diva.
14. Don't ever argue or get defensive when you are given notes by a director, teacher, or in a class critique. The **only** acceptable response to notes is to say thank you and write the note down. You can decide later how you can use it.

These are common-sense items. But you'd be surprised how often common sense is ignored by beginning actors. Get ahead of the curve by listening and learning the rules.

We work so closely with each other in the theatre. Relationships grow quickly and can last a long time because we share deeply with each other on a regular basis. Respect each other and enjoy that. People get "hooked" on doing theatre because there is such expression, such freedom, and such connection with others; that also comes with a responsibility to treat others well.

Inner Life

The performances we really admire are those which make us feel that we've somehow entered completely into the life and mind of a person—that we understand every moment of that character's existence. Actors who succeed at performance often come offstage with the sensation that they have fully lived the experiences of their characters.

Intentional acting helps us to live the experience of a play; but we can do more than that. We can try to understand and duplicate the inner life, or thought process of the character.

How does he think?
What does she hear, see, taste, smell, or touch?
How does each new piece of information which enters his or her brain affect behavior?

THE MOMENTS OF A SCENE: DISCOVERIES AND REALIZATIONS

Everyone has "Aha!" moments in their life, when something becomes suddenly clear. These are important to all human behavior—it changes and expands your understanding of the matter at hand, and often causes a change in your behavior. An example might be the discovery that you are out of gas, or the realization that the stranger coming toward you with a big smile is really your long-lost love who has just come back to town. All good theatrical material has these moments, when a character receives information or gains an understanding that changes things forever. The actor's job is to look for them.

We call these points of discovery the **moments of a scene.** These moments of a scene, a play, or a monologue happen when

1. a character finds out and applies new information, or
2. when she finally understands and applies old information.

As a result of these discoveries or new understandings, the character is forever changed, and the scene or monologue takes a new turn. These "Aha!" moments enhance both the importance and the immediacy of the scene; they **raise the stakes** of the conflict; and—very important—they heighten the experience for both the actor and the audience.

We can break down the acquisition/application of information into two categories:

1. DISCOVERIES—new external information
2. REALIZATIONS—new or resorted internal information.

Discoveries

"Why didn't you tell me before?" Discoveries are the moments when you get information from the outside world which either helps or hurts you in the quest for fulfilling your intention. In plays the discovery usually comes too late or just in the nick of time. This heightens the suspense.

Discovery examples:

> You have been trying to impress someone and a friend comes up to tell you that your fly is unzipped or your blouse is unbuttoned.
> You are rushing to pay an important overdue bill, only to find that the office has been closed due to a family matter.
> You find that a good friend was hurt in the car wreck you just witnessed.

Discoveries involve thinking, but they come in through the senses: something you hear, see, smell, taste, or touch which gives you new information. Much of what we discover comes to us through our eyes—the way someone looks at us, the information in a personal note, the fact that something is NOT where we expected it to be, etc. But we also receive a great deal of information from our ears: words of encouragement or condemnation from another person, the doorbell, the message on an answering machine, a gunshot, etc. The other senses should not be discounted. Think how important the sense of smell is in figuring out that something may be on fire or that someone you love was recently in the room. The sense of taste is key in a scene of seduction which centers around a bottle of fine champagne and chocolate. And the sense of touch must dominate every scene where sexual attraction/repulsion operate or where one person is terrorizing another.

Realizations

"Why didn't I see that before?" Realizations are flashes that hit you when you are putting new information together with information you already possess. Usually this is cumulative; the audience sometimes catches on because they realize the significance of the information before the character does; then part of their pleasure is waiting for the character to catch on, and wondering what will happen when he does.

Oedipus in *Oedipus the King* by Euripides is investigating a murder that happened outside Thebes, the city he rules, only to find that each piece of evidence corresponds exactly with his own experiences before coming to Thebes—he himself is the murderer. By the time he recognizes his guilt, everyone else has seen it coming. (NOTE: Oedipus's pride blinded him—a common malady of comic and tragic heroes. Tragic heroes have to realize that everything they have done to bring about a great action has in fact defeated that action, and themselves in the process.)

Realization example:

> A friend has been helping you over a failed relationship and has even offered to talk to your ex to try and work it out. The next day you see them laughing together. Your friend tells you later that the ex seems to be interested in someone new and that you two probably weren't "meant to be." Your friend becomes increasingly difficult to reach by phone in the evenings. A month later you see them together at a restaurant, having a romantic dinner. "Oh!"

Deeper Realizations "Oh!... Oh!... Oooooh!" The deepest realizations occur when you have to face your true emotions or values. When you make this kind of realization, you see that you must take a certain course of action to be true to your own feelings, values, or beliefs. In most plays, for the sake of dramatic action, these realizations are often in direct contradiction with the character's intention, thus forcing the character to take some unanticipated action.

More Realization Examples:

> A spy realizes that he has fallen in love with a member of the group he has infiltrated.
> A man realizes that he can no longer do his job because he sees how his actions are in direct conflict with his principles.
> Trying to break out of a depression, you realize that you have fallen into a pattern of negative thinking.

Applying Discoveries and Realizations

Here is an example: Let's say that your character left a woman he loved seven years earlier. He has been searching for the woman for several years. When he finally finds her, he is overjoyed and considers how to rekindle the relationship, though both of them have changed considerably in the intervening years. The woman now has a child of about six. Your character finds the child has been named after him, and that the child looks like him. The realization hits that this is HIS son! The woman had never told him about the child! This discovery will strongly affect his actions. Will he be thrilled and want to marry her? Will he feel angry that she never told him? Will he be shaken and need time to process this information? Will he make the decision to nurture a relationship with his son? There are many options, but the stakes here are very high and your character must decide on a course of action. The discovery that he is a father will certainly affect his decisions.

Relationship between Discoveries, Realizations, Obstacles, and Transitions

From what we have learned we know that a character is trying to achieve an intention, and is finding new tactics whenever an obstacle presents itself. How do discoveries and realizations fit into this pattern?

First, let's look at our own behavior. How does an obstacle present itself when you are trying to achieve an intention of your own? It may come externally via an event you witness or an announcement you receive—e.g., when you come into possession of new information. Or the obstacle may be more internal—a moment when you put together information in a new way or when you find out you feel differently about something than you had supposed you would.

In other words, obstacles almost always present themselves as discoveries or realizations. These are the moments—and we all have them—when we have to stop and adjust our behavior to new information and understanding. That's why directors and acting coaches sometimes call these moments "transitions"—something is about to change.

If you are genuinely following the thought process of the character and constantly measuring your progress toward the achievement of your intention, you will find that you need a transitional moment to register information and make adjustments in your tactics.

Some discoveries and realizations will be small transitions; some will be life-changing (like the example of discovering a child you had not known about). In real life, you make a key realization and you change the entire direction of your actions and/or behavior. If you realize that you are spending too much time with a friend who is involving you in a lifestyle which is wrong for you, you would probably decide not to see that "friend" any longer and to get back on track to a healthy lifestyle. In much the same way, in a play the large realizations (those which change the entire course of the character's tactical path) will probably also be the "great moments" of the play or scene—the ones which the audience will remember for a long time. These are pivotal moments in the lives of the primary characters and, as such, affect everything that happens in the world of the play.

Therefore, the sequence of behavior is this: the discovery or realization reveals obstacles and forces a change of tactics. The new tactic begins after this transition has occurred; this begins the next action.

As an actor, you will want to find all of the viable discoveries and realizations you can, because they will spark interesting choices and enrich your performance. They will also increase your believability and involve your audience's empathy. If you can find and play these moments truthfully, they will add depth and reality to your role.

TRUTH IN ACTION—STAY IN THE MOMENT

It's tempting to get ahead of yourself in a scene because you already know how it ends. But the character doesn't know what is going to happen; she is desperately trying everything at hand to affect the outcome of the situation in her favor. Remember that and do everything you can to keep the play happening moment-to-moment, or as actors like to say: "Stay in the moment." If you find your mind projecting ahead to your lines or the upcoming action, you are not "in the moment."

So how do you get to "the moment" and stay there?
You listen carefully to your partner for clues as to your (character's) needs.
You fully involve yourself in each action of the scene as it comes up.
You evaluate everything that happens in terms of your intention.
You rehearse the details of the scene (lines, blocking, physical action, etc.) over and over again, so that you don't need to be thinking about those things at all.

Another way to look at this idea of staying in the moment is, as previously mentioned, to remember that your character has no clear idea of what is going to happen next; while you (the actor), of course, have rehearsed the scene and know everything that will happen. But for your character, each next line, each next action, is something new. It will change what the character does next, but the character cannot do that next thing (or anticipate it) until the present action has been done. Each moment has to take place before the character can go on. In fact, the present moment has to happen before the character can even decide what to do to go on. Stay in the moment, see what it brings, then—because of what happens in this moment—move on to the next action and dialogue, the next moment.

Of course there will be one little part of your brain which is thinking about the actual here-and-now (theatre, audience, and fellow actors). Sometimes, it's a larger part. What if the set is falling down over there? What if your scene is about a letter and the "prop" letter is not where it's supposed to be? What if your partner forgets his lines? In those cases you trust your instincts, improvise, and get the scene back to its main action as soon as you can. But your performance will be more truthful (and more satisfying to you) if you can concentrate on creating the world of the play (in the character's head) instead of concentrating on lines and props and scenery.

Moment Before

One way to make sure that you are as connected as possible with the character's intention, aware of the given circumstances, and in tune with your partner, is to work the **moment before** of your scene in rehearsal. Let's assume you are working on a scene and your part begins with an entrance. To work the "moment before," you take the time before you enter to work out the following things:

What just happened to me immediately *before* this scene starts?
Where am I coming from?
Why did I decide to come here?
What have I just heard?
What have I just seen (tasted, smelled, touched)?
What am I thinking about as I make my entrance?

Now turn your attention to all of the information you are gathering as you walk into the room.

Who was I expecting to see? Who do I see?
Is this place okay? Do I feel comfortable here?
What do I need to do? (intention)
Are there any obstacles?
What should I do first?

Do the first couple of lines of the scene and debrief with your partner. Are you "anticipating"? That means you are aware of information that you shouldn't have yet and this knowledge is influencing your performance. An example would be if your character enters the room with anger, *before* he has been told that his money is missing. He cannot act angry until he reacts to the new information. You must be sure that you are really listening and seeing what is going on around you. Do you enter the room with a different expectation, and then *hear* the new information and react **in the moment?** Or are you being lazy by *anticipating* that you will soon be angry, as you enter? There is no doubt that the audience can tell the difference, and will no longer believe your performance if you are not listening before you react.

If you are not entering into the scene, but are already onstage when the scene begins, you can still ask all of the above questions. They are even valid if your scene begins in the middle of an interchange with another person. No matter what the circumstances, you will need to go back a bit to establish context and to get yourself thinking the character's thoughts.

Once you get into the habit of creating the moment before in preparation for every scene that you do, you will connect to your characters more easily and clearly. And it's a necessary step to make sure that you and your partner are on the same wavelength from the beginning.

SUBTEXT AND HOW TO FIND IT

One of the best ways to figure out what is going on in a scene is to figure out what the characters are really saying. This isn't always simple. Like people, characters often say one thing and mean something entirely different. For instance, a character may say, "Gee, I'm really glad to see you." This sounds innocuous enough, but the character might really mean any of the following things:

"Oh brother, I was hoping I'd never see you again."
"I really missed you."
"Why didn't you call?"
"You look wonderful."
" Oh! You surprised me, I wish you hadn't walked in right now."

What the characters say out loud is their dialogue or text. What they are saying underneath their lines is called their subtext. The subtext is what you have to figure out before you can decide on the central dramatic action of the scene.

It can be difficult to discover the subtext within a character's dialogue, but it is essential to do so. For one thing, subtext in plays is similar to subtext in real life. People with simple, straightforward personalities who are being simple, direct, and honest tend not to use a lot of subtext. That is, what they say is pretty much what they mean. However, complex people, or people in complex situations—often social situations—consciously say things that differ from what they really mean. This applies to most characters in most modern, realistic drama.

In investigating your character's text/subtext dialogue, consider how direct and blunt he or she is trying to be at this moment. Is there an intention to withhold, to conceal, to be sneaky, to manipulate or be sarcastic? Is there any sign the character might be trying to be subtle, to use tact and diplomacy, to avoid hurting someone's feelings? In cases such as any of these, there is almost certain to be a subtext to the actual dialogue the character is saying.

In addition, dialogue needs to be performed in a way that lets the audience know there is subtext; that the character is doing more, or less, or different than he is saying. This almost always comes in the form of how you speak: vocal pattern, tone, pitch, and rate are all consciously manipulated when you are using subtext. The way you change your tone is how you tell your listener you are using subtext.

CHAPTER SEVEN EXERCISES

1. Rehearse saying several of the following sentences out loud. Practice them until you can say each with at least two different meanings. An example would be saying "Oh, that's a nice dress." Say it once as though you really mean it. Now, try saying it as though you think the dress is horrible, but are trying to protect the girl's feelings. Consciously alter your vocal pattern to make each subtext meaning clear. Once you have practiced, try the sentences below on a partner, asking that person to tell you what you actually meant each time. Don't be afraid to try different subtexts. Note inflection and vocal tone changes that occur with each different subtext.

   "That is a really nice car you bought."
   "Who was that guy I saw you with last night?"
   "Would you like to come to the movies with me?"
   "I've never seen a dog like that before."
   "Boy, I really enjoyed this evening."

   In each case you ought to have made strong dramatic choices for your meanings, and your partner should have been able to get pretty clearly what you were trying to do. Did it work?

2. Now let's try working on subtext in a written script, "Espresso Bar," by Kristin McKague.[1] This short script is full of subtext. The two characters meet after having not seen each other for awhile. They seem to have had some sort of relationship in the past. They have a short, apparently trivial conversation. But is the scene about more than what appears on the surface? Yes.

   Read the scene, and then propose three different underlying meanings for the scene. In other words, think about the possibilities for given circumstances (much as you did for the content-less scenes) and then evaluate if these possibilities might work with the text. Write down three different scenarios: what the characters' relationship was, why they parted, and what they want from each other now:

   1. _____

   2. _____

   3. _____

Compare these with another person's interpretations. Try to back up your ideas by going back to the text. Then talk about what the subtext might be for each line.

Remember, one of the great freedoms an actor has is in his or her determination of subtext; but you do have a responsibility to respect what the author has written. Professional actors read over their scripts daily to find new insights and try many approaches to their lines to get the most out of every word. This kind of detective work is crucial to good acting.

---

[1]"Espresso Bar" is printed with the permission of the author, Kristin McKague, and can be found in Appendix A.

Creating the Inner Life of the Character

Your challenge is to get inside the actions, the body, and the mind of your character. A good place to begin is with intention and relationships. Finding "as ifs," looking for discoveries and realizations, determining character dynamics, playing around with subtext, trying out the moment before—all of these are good strong tools to help you develop a full inner life for your character.

CHAPTER SEVEN EXERCISES

1. Do a subtext rehearsal.
   a. Go through the rehearsal saying what the character is thinking out loud, not just what they say in the script.
   b. Debrief with your partner afterwards and find out what new information or changes in interpretation came from the subtext rehearsal.

2. Try the Knee-to-Knee Rehearsal found at the end of Chapter 6 and add the following:
   a. Mark in pencil in your photocopied script the places where your character changes tactics (transitions).
   b. Also mark discoveries and realizations.

Monologues—Telling the Story

Any scene that you create, rehearse, and perform contains all the elements of any acting task. First, and most important, you figure out what is really going on in the scene. In any scene, the words are only the top level of what is going on; it is always the actor's job to look through, behind, and beneath the words to discover what is happening that makes the character need to say the specific words that the script provides. As you now know, every word the character says stems from the character's strong need to achieve his or her intention, and the character is always using specific tactics to overcome the obstacles that pop up during the scene.

Many scenes are dialogues—two or more characters onstage at once, each trying to accomplish his intention in the face of the obstacles that the other character(s) present. Sometimes a character gives a long, uninterrupted speech with other characters present. Other times, however, the character is onstage alone, speaking aloud. These solitary speeches—called monologues, or sometimes soliloquies in older plays—present all the same acting tasks that you find in any scene. In a monologue, the character is trying to achieve an intention in the face of one or more obstacles, using tactics. The first thing, as always, is to determine why the character is talking aloud—what the character's intention is.

THE INTENTIONS OF A MONOLOGUE

Like all other lines spoken onstage, the lines in a monologue come from a character's need to accomplish something. She may need to:

- figure something out;
- explain why she did a certain thing;
- convince or persuade somebody else to do something;
- tell the story of something important that happened so that someone else
    - understands, or
    - forgives, or
    - rewards her.

Monologues are an important part of acting, but beginning actors often find them difficult because it doesn't seem natural to talk for a long time. Really, though, a monologue is just telling a story that's important to the character, and telling it so that other people understand both the story and why it's important.

If you look at a monologue as telling an important story and making someone understand it and why it's important to you, then you already know how to do it. In your life, you, like everybody, have had several important things happen to you, and you can tell those stories naturally and convincingly. Some of your stories are funny, some of them are sad, and some of them are dramatic, but they're all important stories to you, and when you tell them, you do so for a reason: again, to convince, persuade, explain, or because you need them to understand, forgive or reward you (entertaining them so that they "reward" you with laughter counts, too). So, you already have several monologues in your personal history that you can share with people. (See personal monologue exercise at the end of the chapter.)

Moving the Audience

When you are doing a monologue, your intention is to make your partner understand you better or give you what you want. If you communicate clearly to your partner, you will communicate clearly to your audience. The same criteria apply. All we look for is the truth of your story. Do you believe it? Is it important to you? Can you take us where you are (or where you were, if it's a memory monologue)?

Why Do a Monologue?

Some actors find monologues difficult—for these reasons:

> It's hard to talk to someone who's not there.
> You have to create your own emotional energy.
> There is no one creating an obstacle to your intention, so you have to create that too.

Many actors love monologues—for these reasons:
> You can work a monologue all by yourself, without having to depend on another person's availability.
> Monologues make great audition pieces.
>> You can show a lot of range (emotionally and concerning your "type") with a set of two contrasting (comedic/dramatic) monologues back to back.
>> You are the featured performer in the monologue.

SCORING

When an actor prepares a scene or monologue, one of the things they do is to *score* the text. What does this accomplish and why do actors bother to do this? Scoring provides a "roadmap" that they can follow (and adjust) as they work on a piece of text. As they begin to make decisions about the text, they make notations on the script with symbols to pinpoint exactly where tactics change, discoveries and realizations occur, where the character may pause to think or react, which lines contain subtext, where changes in pace may cause the tension in a scene to build, or where an obstacle is encountered by the character, etc.

This notation is always done in pencil, so that any new insights an actor has later, as he continues to rehearse, can be incorporated, and the "road signs" can be changed or adjusted as needed. By marking these important moments, an actor can go back to his script at any time and see what his previous decisions were, the last time he worked on the script. Then, he can choose to keep or change things, in order to further develop the character. With this "roadmap," an actor won't forget what happened in the last rehearsal, or any important insights they had while working on the text. It also formulates the character's thought pattern, making memorization much easier—instead of a random collection of sentences, there is now a logical sequence of *cause and effect*, that motivates each word a character says. It is easiest to demonstrate this method of notation on a monologue.

MIKE'S MONOLOGUE

Here is a monologue from *Lovers and Other Strangers* by Taylor and Bologna.[1] We have printed the text as it exists in the acting script. This is a great monologue example for an actor to score. Read it carefully; then we'll try the scoring process on it.

(Mike starts to leave and then comes back to Susan.) I'm not getting married! . . . I said, "I'm not getting married!" . . . I told you this would happen? . . . I told you I wasn't ready. Do you remember? I said,

---

[1]From *Lovers and Other Strangers*. Copyright 1968 by Renee Taylor and Joseph Bologna. Reprinted with permission of the authors.

"Susan, if I ask you to marry me, can I take it back if I want to?" And you said I could, didn't you? . . . Well, I'm taking it back now. I mean it's not that I don't love you, because I love you. I really love you, Susan, but it just can't be for keeps. I tried, Susan, I really tried, but it's getting close. There's only four days left. Just four more days and I can't go any further. . . . No, sir. No, ma'am. Uh–uh. No chance. No, siree. . . . Uh–uh. That's it. I can't do it. That's it!

Please don't make me marry you! I know this wedding is costing your parents a lot of money, but I'll pay back every penny of it. . . . Look, I've got about twenty dollars on me. Here, take it as a deposit . . . and take my watch . . . and I want you to keep the ring. I know when a fella breaks up with a girl, he's supposed to get the ring back, but you can have the ring. That's fair, isn't it? I mean, another guy wouldn't do that, would he, Susan?

Please stop looking at me like that. You shouldn't take it personally. It's nothing against you. It's the times we live in. India's overpopulated! We'll all be sterilized soon. The suicide rate is up. The air is polluted. Is that the kind of world you want to get married in? Is it, Susan? Is it? . . . I know what you're trying to do—make me look like the bad one. Well, it won't work. It won't work. Because I'm clean. I'm clean. You knew exactly what you were doing. You knew I was a confirmed bachelor. You knew I had trouble getting involved, but that didn't stop you. No, not you, baby. You decided to marry me and that was it. Well, who do you think you are, playing God with another person's life? Well, I have no pity for you. None whatsoever, because you're getting just what you deserve. So, get off my back. I owe you nothing, baby. Get it? I owe you nothing!

Give me a break. Take the pressure off me. Call the wedding off. Everything was going along great. We were having fun and smelling flowers. We could go on having fun for years. . . . And then some day maybe I'll have a lot of drinks and we could just sneak down to City Hall. That way I won't feel like I'm married. What do you say, Susan? Huh, Susan? What do you say?

All right, Susan. I've got to put my cards on the table. I didn't want to tell you this because I didn't want to hurt your feelings. You're just not my dream girl. I'm sorry. I wish you were, but let's face it, Susan. My heart doesn't beat when you come into a room. I don't get goose pimples when I touch you. I'm just not nervous when I'm with you. You're too vulnerable. You're too human. You've got too many problems. And, Susan, there's something about you that really bother me. Maybe it wouldn't be important to another guy, but I think about it a lot. Susan, you have very thin arms.

So, I don't think I could faithful. I mean, I want to be faithful, but I just don't think I can. Ever since we got engaged, I walk down the street and I want to grab every ass I see. That's not normal. If you were my dream girl, I'd never give other women a second thought. Don't you understand? I need somebody more perfect, then it wouldn't be so much work for me to love and be faithful. I could just show up.

Look, you'll get over me. After a while, you'll find another boy. Just promise me you won't sleep with anyone until you get married. Will you promise me that, Susan? Will you?

That's it. It's all over. (He picks up her hand and shakes it.) Goodbye, I'm sorry. That's it.

(Below we have included the rest of the scene to help you understand the complete context of this monologue.)

(Pause.)

SUSAN: Did you and your father pick up the tuxedos today?

MIKE: Yeah.

SUSAN: Did you get the cuff links for the ushers?

MIKE: Yeah.

SUSAN: Wait 'til you see the beautiful salad bowl we got from Tom and Betty. It's from Tiffany's.

MIKE: No kidding? By the way, my mother called and said we forgot to seat my Uncle John from Boston.

SUSAN: I think we can put him at table number three.

MIKE: Did your wedding gown come?

SUSAN: Yes. Wait 'til you see it.

MIKE: I'll bet it's pretty.

SUSAN: Yes. Yes.

(Lights fade.) CURTAIN.

SCORING MIKE'S MONOLOGUE

When you start to work on a monologue from a pre-written play instead of from your own experience, you begin by performing the same analytical operations that you do on any other piece of dramatic material. You already know that you need to read the play carefully, and find specific things. For the monologue itself you will need to find the character's intention, determine the obstacle(s), isolate the different tactics, realizations and discoveries, figure out relationships and the inner life of the character. Looking at the monologue carefully to learn what the character's train of thought is and how he moves through the process of the speech will also help you put this together.

Using a notation system to document your work on the speech is called **scoring**. This is a system of putting your analytical work right into the script; having notes in the script itself helps you organize your thoughts as you rehearse. You can keep track of any new insights you get during rehearsal. *Scoring indicates the sequence of choices the actor is making about the monologue or scene.*

If you continue to act, you will probably develop a system of your own to help you break apart your script. Until you do, this is a sample of the method by which many professional actors incorporate their analytical work into a "working script." (We call it a "working script" because you have all your notes to work from, right in the script you are rehearsing with.) It is best to begin with a copy of the text of your monologue before you mark an actual script until you get the hang of it. Be sure to leave some room on the left for notes about obstacles, tactics, discoveries, and realizations. You will add your notes in that blank space as you score the script.

Intention, Obstacles, and Tactics

Start out by figuring out Mike's intention. What does he want or need? Everything he says and does should lead you to understand what he is trying to get. Look for the obstacles. What gets in his way as he proceeds through the action of the monologue? Remember that there are internal and external obstacles. Once you have identified your working intention and have begun to determine obstacles, you will be ready to look for Mike's major tactics. (Reminder: Active verbs make for exciting acting choices; they are stronger and much easier to support.)

It's important to remember when tackling a monologue that the character does not intend to give a monologue when he starts a speech. He says one thing (statement or question), and when he doesn't get a response, he goes on to say the next thing. Each set of things he says is a further attempt to achieve his intention. The reason he says anything at all after the first sentence is that he can tell (by what the partner is doing) that he hasn't gotten what he wants or needs; the partner doesn't get it. Therefore, in order to achieve the intention, he'll have to try something else. In other words, when he realizes that his current tactic isn't working, he modifies it or tries a new one.

Mike's **intention:** to get Susan to call off the wedding.

Obstacles: She loves him. She won't accept any of his excuses. He is too chicken to call it off himself. He really loves her a lot. His excuses sound pretty flimsy even to him. Every time he looks at her he realizes that he needs her.

Remember to write the intention and obstacles in pencil so that you can adjust them as you work the monologue in rehearsal. Make clear choices, try them out with conviction, and then adjust to what works best for you and the character. Find the strongest possible choices.

Given Circumstances

Now we need to figure out the given circumstances for Mike's monologue.

Where do you find the necessary information to determine the **given circumstances** for the context of a monologue? You will not find all the information you need about the character, the situation, and the other given circumstances in the monologue itself, so you must go back to look carefully at the rest of the play (for our purposes here, the given circumstances will be outlined below). What information applies to the immediate situation in the monologue? Make some notes at the beginning or ending of your script so that you will keep these points in mind as you create the scene.

Given circumstances for Mike's Monologue: Mike and Susan are supposed to get married in a few days. They are in her apartment, it's four in the morning, Mike is "just passing by." He is actually getting a bad case of cold feet. Susan recognizes this and patiently listens to him as he tries to get out of the wedding.

Context is critical. It is always important to know every detail about the play you're working with. Otherwise you could really blow it by making incorrect assumptions, or missing crucial information. Knowing, for instance, that a character runs away at the end of the play, or that the wife has had an affair before the scene in question makes a big difference to a character's strategic position at the time of a monologue.

Tactics and Actions

After you've figured out the given circumstances and the intention and obstacles, you can begin to see a train of thought which drives the monologue. You do this in Mike's monologue by locating where he changes his tactics. Once you know where the tactics change, you must then figure out what causes the character to change them. Put a mark or draw a line wherever you think the character has changed tactics. This delineation signifies a new course of action. Often a tactic change is preceded by a realization that the current tactic is not working.

Mike's scored monologue follows with **tactic changes and new actions** marked by lines. In this model of a scored monologue we have put the actor notes in the margin because it's more accessible during rehearsal or while studying the script. The intention goes at the top. Remember that the intention seldom changes (only if the ceiling falls in, someone gets shot, or something equally earth-shattering), but that if it does, you would make a larger break in the script and put the new intention in the proper place. You may develop another system of symbols which create a clearer picture for you; meanwhile, see how this system works as a place for you to start.

T=Tactic, D=Discovery, R=Realization, and O=Obstacle, ******* = Tactic Change

Mike's Monologue Scored Sample Section 1.

Intention: to get Susan to call off the wedding

1. T: to lay down the law
    D: she isn't responding
    O: her disbelief

    ****: Tactic change

2. T: to reassure her of his love without commit-
        ting too much
    O: his love for her
    D: her hurt feelings
    ****: Tactic change

3. T: to get her to see how hard it is for him
    O: she doesn't agree with him
    R: it's getting close!

    ****: Tactic change

4. T: to plead with her for his freedom
    D&O: that she isn't going to make this easy
    ****: Tactic change

5. T: to bargain with her
    O: lack of money
    R: he doesn't want her to give up the ring he
    gave her

    ****: Tactic change

6. T: to put the blame on a third party
    D: she's beginning to hurt
    R: he knows he's being a chump
    O: weak argument

****: Tactic change

(Mike starts to leave and then comes back to Susan.)

1. I'm not getting married! . . .
    I said, "I'm not getting married!" . . . I told you this would happen . . . I told you I wasn't ready. Do you remember? I said, "Susan, if I ask you to marry me, can I take it back if I want to?" And you said I could, didn't you? . . . Well, I'm taking it back now.
    ****

2. I mean it's not that I don't love you, because I love you. I really love you, Susan, but it just can't be for keeps.
    ****

3. I tried, Susan, I really tried, but it's getting close. There's only four days left. Just four more days and I can't go any further. . . . No, sir. No, ma'am. Uh-uh. No chance. No, siree. . . . Uh-uh. That's it. I can't do it. That's it!
    ****

4. Please don't make me marry you! I know this wedding is costing your parents a lot of money, but I'll pay back every penny of it.
    ****

5. Look, I've got about twenty dollars on me. Here, take it as a deposit . . . and take my watch . . . and I want you to keep the ring. I know when a fella breaks up with a girl, he's supposed to get the ring back, but you can have the ring. That's fair, isn't it? I mean, another guy wouldn't do that, would he, Susan?
    ****

6. Please stop looking at me like that. You shouldn't take it personally. It's nothing against you. It's the times we live in. India's overpopulated! We'll all be sterilized soon. The suicide rate is up. The air is polluted. Is that the kind of world you want to get married in? Is it, Susan? Is it?
    ****

7. T: to paint Susan as the bad guy and himself as the victim
   D: she is smiling at him!
   R: he is going to have to get rough here
   O: he knows she's no villain

****: Tactic change

8. T: to plead with her to postpone the wedding a while
   D: her incredulous expression
   O: his sense of fairness and love for her
   R: he really wants to marry her

****Tactic change

9. T: to list her flaws and make her see how they are incompatible
   O: she won't play the game
   D: her shock
   R: that he's being cruel

****Tactic change

10. T: to admit his own flaws in the sexual area
    O: his embarrassment at revealing her flaws to her

****: Tactic change

7. I know what you're trying to do—make me look like the bad one. Well, it won't work. It won't work. Because I'm clean. I'm clean. You knew exactly what you were doing. You knew I was a confirmed bachelor. You knew I had trouble getting involved, but that didn't stop you. No, not you, baby. You decided to marry me and that was it. Well, who do you think you are, playing God with another person's life? Well, I have no pity for you. None whatsoever, because you're getting just what you deserve. So, get off my back. I owe you nothing, baby. Get it? I owe you nothing!
   ****

8. Give me a break. Take the pressure off me. Call the wedding off. Everything was going along great. We were having fun and smelling flowers. We could go on having fun for years. . . . And then some day maybe I'll have a lot of drinks and we could just sneak down to City Hall. That way I won't feel like I'm married. What do you say, Susan? Huh, Susan? What do you say?
   ****

9. All right, Susan. I've got to put my cards on the table. I didn't want to tell you this because I didn't want to hurt your feelings. You're just not my dream girl. I'm sorry. I wish you were, but let's face it, Susan. My heart doesn't beat when you come into a room. I don't get goose pimples when I touch you. I'm just not nervous when I'm with you. You're too vulnerable. You're too human. You've got too many problems. And, Susan, there's something about you that really bothers me. Maybe it wouldn't be important to another guy, but I think about it a lot. Susan, you have very thin arms.
   ****

10. So, I don't think I could faithful. I mean, I want to be faithful, but I just don't think I can. Ever since we got engaged, I walk down the street and I want to grab every ass I see. That's not normal. If you were my dream girl, I'd never give other women a second thought. Don't you understand? I need somebody more perfect, then it wouldn't be so much work for me to love and be faithful. I could just show up.
    ****

11. T: to make himself feel better about losing her
O: his growing conviction that he's being a heel
R: that she'll sleep with someone else!
****: Tactic change

11. Look, you'll get over me. After a while, you'll find another boy. Just promise me you won't sleep with anyone until you get married. Will you promise me that, Susan? Will you?

****

12. T: to set calling off the wedding in stone as their course of action
D: she's still not going to say anything
O: she has not agreed with him on anything
R: he has failed to achieve his intention

12. That's it. It's all over. (He picks up her hand and shakes it.) Goodbye, I'm sorry. That's it.

Review of Scoring Formula

1. Examine intention, tactics, and relationship: Read the monologue out loud. What is Mike doing (in each line)? What response is he getting from Susan? How does this response cause him to change tactics? What immediate goal is he trying to accomplish with each new tactic? Keep in mind that, at every point, Mike is always trying to achieve his intention, so an immediate goal would be, for example, "to get her to agree" or "to shock her out of her goal" (i.e., to marry Mike). When one tactic doesn't work he goes on to another one.

2. Find the given circumstances. Read the monologue within the context of the rest of the play. What brings Mike to this point? What has happened that influences or motivates Mike to say these things, and to *need* to accomplish his intention?

3. Read the monologue out loud again. Find the tactic changes (indicate them by drawing a line). Notice that the action changes whenever the tactic changes. Look for the corresponding goal for each action. A good way to evaluate is to think of tactics in this manner: every tactic has 2 parts: an action and a goal. The goal is related to the intention, but is generally a smaller step, grounded in the moment. Example: Mike leaves and then comes back *(action) in order to say* "I'm not getting married!" *(goal)*. When you write out the tactic, use the phrase "in order to" to link the action to the (immediate) goal, and you will be on the right track. However, there are times a character uses several versions of the same action, within a single tactic. Example: Mike describes *many* of Susan's flaws *(action)* in order to show her that they are incompatible *(goal)*.

   Read the monologue out loud a third time. Notice where your inflection changes or where there is a new topic. (Sometimes the way the playwright uses paragraphs will help you in this.) The place where you see, hear, or feel a change is usually where the new tactic begins. You will start to find the places where the next tactic begins, with practice (look for a new topic, an emotional switch, or a response to a major realization or discovery).

4. Realizations/discoveries and obstacles: Make notes for the realizations/discoveries and obstacles which play a part in this scoring process too. Whenever a character makes a discovery (external information received), or has a realization (internal reprocessing of information), it affects the success of his intention. For example, if Mike discovers that Susan is laughing at him (obstacle), it means that his tactic is not working and that he'd better change it. If he realizes that his justification is pretty lame, that's also an obstacle—an internal one—and he'd better come up with a better tactic. Discoveries can confirm tactics as well. For example, after he begins, he discovers that she is not responding, so he reminds her (in order to achieve his intention) that he said this would happen.

5. After you've analyzed and "scored" the monologue, you would memorize the speech using your notes. Then you would invest it with emotional importance, keeping the stakes high. You would rehearse it carefully, taking care to advocate for your character. Finally, you will fully commit to the actual performance.

The Point of the Monologue

As you work on a monologue, you will find out why this monologue is necessary and important to the character. Therefore, one of the final things you do when analyzing a monologue or scene is to try to figure out what the character is driving toward, or what is the most important thing that he says. When you understand this, the whole monologue falls into place, because you know where you're going and can thus make intelligent choices about what to emphasize, what you can "throw away," and what you must be sure to communicate clearly and strongly. (In theatre terms, "throwing away" is not meant literally—it means saying some lines lightly or casually, rather than giving them primary emphasis. You would give a very strange performance indeed, if *every* line was said with strong emphasis: they would all sound the same!)

This has more to do with the way the monologue is written, i.e., its structure, than with its content. A good playwright will plan the building of the monologue so that it has maximum impact on the audience.

Sometimes the character will say the most important thing first, and the rest of the monologue explains what he is talking about. This is what Hamlet does in his famous speech that begins "O that this too, too solid flesh would melt, thaw, and resolve itself into a dew." He wishes he didn't exist, because things are so terrible for him. Sometimes the important statement comes at the end of the speech. There is no set place, and definitely no "right" placement, for the point of the speech. But wherever it comes, you must be able to spot it and drive your speech toward it.

USING THE FORMULA FOR SCORING A MONOLOGUE

Now it's your turn. When you work on your assigned or chosen monologue, do the following steps.

1. Decide what the character is trying to get or do. The main possibilities:
    *   figure something out;
    *   explain why she did a certain thing;
    *   convince or persuade somebody else to do something;
    *   tell the story of something important that happened so that:
        someone else understands or forgives or rewards him.

2. Score the monologue. Try out some intentions and settle on a working intention. (See if the ones above help you out.) Find the changes in action. Determine the obstacles and tactics. Figure out where the realizations and discoveries are. How and where does the partner react? Confirm your intention or, if it doesn't quite fit, change it and start over. Label all of these on your script.

    Remember, some of the strongest material is touchy. Make bold choices and share your true feelings. Passive choices (acting "bored" or ignoring the other character) are not compelling for the audience to watch—you will lose their interest.

3. Make the language your own. Don't rewrite the author's words, but go over your monologue until you understand how the character talks, in terms of the words he or she uses and how he or she constructs the tactics or remembers the story.

4. Attach what your character is describing to authentic emotional responses from your self. There are two main ways to do this:
    a. Find an incident in your own life that is similar and respond to the story the character is telling with your own reactions; or
    b. Find a good "as if." "How would I feel if this were happening to me?" "What experiences do I have which I can bring to bear on this?" "What would a clear parallel experience be in my own life?"
5. Memorize your lines, *and* your character's train of thought, as well as the tactics that he uses. Figure out the point of the monologue.
6. Rehearse your monologue, trying as hard as you can to get what your character wants from the partner in the scene.
7. Perform it, trying to get from your partner the appropriate responses. Heighten the stakes and achieve your intention! Or, if the play calls for your character to fail to achieve his intention (as in Mike's monologue), you must still fight as hard as you can, until that final moment when he realizes that he has lost.

Putting It All Together

This may seem like a ponderous set of tasks to perform for a short speech. If you don't do it, however, you will be winging it on instinct and very possibly look foolish, when you could instead be confidently executing your analysis. A good analogy would be trying to drive in a strange town without a map: it *might* work, but there is also a very real possibility you'll get lost. Following a map will give you a much better chance of arriving at your destination. Scoring is a carefully planned "map" through your scene or monologue. When you really understand what the character is trying to do and how they set about accomplishing their goals, it will become much easier for you to perform successfully.

The Payoff

First, after you've done all the analytical steps described above, you'll find that you have already memorized most of the monologue, without even trying. The rest of it will be easy to learn, because you'll be learning your lines in terms of your character's train of thought, and not just as a set of unrelated words. If your memory should fail you on the specific word you need, you'll know what the character's trying to do and where he or she is in the process; so you'll be able to ad lib, if necessary, to get yourself back on track with the author's words. Actors who learn speeches using this train-of-thought method rarely ever get into serious trouble with lines, because they know their characters so well that they can fill in until the right words come to them.

Second, if you do all this analysis and really understand what your character is saying and what it means to him, you'll be able to find parallels in your own life—your own "as ifs." Then you can make the speech matter to your character because you will really identify with what's happening inside the character. You will find that character advocacy—seeing things from your character's point of view—simply isn't a problem. When you know someone really well, you understand that person and can advocate strongly for him or her.

Third, if you have done all this homework thoroughly and honestly, you will be able to bring passion, commitment, energy, and confidence to your performance. When you understand the tactics that your character uses to achieve her intention, and how her train of thought progresses, it becomes easy to get up and just go for it.

CHAPTER EIGHT EXERCISES

The Personal Monologue

1. Pick a story from your own life. Begin by jotting down three or four of the most important things that have happened to you in your life. Your strongest memories are a good place to start. Think of things that truly changed your life, or that made a big difference to you, or that made you understand things in new ways.

   IMPORTANT NOTE: Be sure that you choose something that you can share with others. Don't choose an unhealed hurt, or anything that you feel would be inappropriate to tell the class. Remember that acting is sharing some emotional experience that you understand with others; it is not therapy or a place to dump all your grief, frustration, anger, etc. It needn't be tragic—think of your happiest moment, or the first time you fell in love, or someone who taught you something really important that changed your life for the better.

2. Tell the story to a tape recorder—THIS STEP IS CRUCIAL—Do not skip over it. The reason for tape-recording your story, rather than writing it down, is that you want to hear it exactly as you would tell it to someone, spontaneously, the way you actually talk. Keep all the pauses, even the "ums", incorrect grammar, hesitations, clearing your throat, laughing, whatever. It should be honest and real, not structured and edited. Keep it short, no longer than 1 page or 2 minutes.

3. Type up the script. Transcribe your story by typing it *exactly* as you spoke it, putting in all the "hmmms" and "errrs," etc. Don't worry if it doesn't sound fancy. You want to end up with the story that you know well, in the exact words you used to tell it.

4. Pick a partner from class and read your story aloud. Let them give you honest reactions. If there is something your partner notices that lessens the impact of the story (repetitions, or missing a piece of information, necessary for understanding), you may change that before memorizing it, but only cut or add the minimum. Try to retain everything in your original story, as much as possible.

5. Memorize your story exactly. You should have an easy time, because you already *know* the story that you're telling. Memorize by learning your story, not just by learning the lines mechanically. Memorize what you have transcribed, word for word, including all the vocal elements (again: include pauses, laughter, ums, hmms, etc.).

6. Tell your story to the class. Don't act. Tell them sincerely. Remember your story; see it as it happened; run that "movie" behind your eyes. Tell your story with the intention to make your audience understand you better, to understand what happened to you. You are trying to affect the audience with your own truth. If you can't affect them with *your* truth, you will never be able to do it with someone else's (the playwright, or the character in the play). You must first learn how to do it with your own experiences.

Chapter 9

Scoring the Scene

In the previous chapter you learned how to break apart a monologue so that you could work it in rehearsal. The principles you learned (about finding an intention, picking out the obstacles, choosing strong tactics, and identifying the discoveries and realizations) apply to scene work as well.

When you are given a scene to perform, you need to read the play carefully. Then, begin to do specific detective work. A detective takes notes about "clues," looks at the various meanings of those clues, and ponders the connections. The actor considers all possible scenarios, subtext and meanings, importance and possibilities within the script, contemplating the best choices. An actor must do certain things to prepare any role: get information (from the script directly, but also from research into the time period, location, culture, social customs, manners, taboos, etc.), take notes, ponder connections, figure out all possible scenarios, and decide upon the strongest choices. When actors work on a scene, they read the script and work with scene partners in rehearsal. By pondering connections and considering the strongest possibilities, an actor decides the best way to play the scene. There is always more to learn about the characters we play; it is up to us to do the work.

NOTETAKING

Notetaking for actors is very personalized. Some actors have a separate journal for rehearsal notes and reactions to script-readings. Some actors use tape recorders for debriefing. But many actors take notes right in their scripts so they can refer to them even while they are in the middle of rehearsal. The best actors can often be found after a rehearsal, going over their notes and making adjustments. These actors value the time to rethink their roles and rethink the scene according to valuable new insights they got during the rehearsal.

What do they write in their scripts? The basics: Intention for the play, intention for the scene, the major obstacles as they occur, tactics to circumvent these obstacles, and any discoveries or realizations. (Actors also usually include blocking and any special notes that they wish to remember.)

When scoring scene, you will use the same technique as for the monologue, but you will only score *your* character's intentions, obstacles, tactics, discoveries, and realizations. Your scene partner will score his or hers. Do not let differences in interpretations become stumbling blocks, impeding your progress. Instead, keep an open mind and a collaborative attitude. Consider your partner's interpretations as just as valid as yours. Take the time to try the scene in a number of different interpretations, and see how well each interpretation works. Don't be afraid to combine elements of differing interpretations; you may come up with a *very* interesting and engaging performance.

POINTS TO REMEMBER AS YOU EXAMINE AND SCORE YOUR ASSIGNED SCENES

1. Every actor or actress will approach the scene slightly different and get different insights from a scene. Therefore, you may or may not agree with every interpretation of a given scene, but you will still learn a great deal about the *process* of scoring by reading each step carefully.

Remember: do not judge another actor's interpretations negatively. Listen carefully and see if you can ADD what your partner comes up with to your own interpretation. Often, this approach will strengthen it.

2. In the left column, next to the text of the script, T is for Tactics, O is for Obstacle, D is for Discovery, and R is for Realization. Always put the intention for the scene at the top of the scene (or at the point where your character enters the scene).

3. There is usually only one intention for the scene, and that intention relates directly to the intention the character has for the whole play. (Remember the nesting concept we introduced in Chapter 4?) Check to make sure that all of the tactics in the scene relate directly to the intention of the scene and advance the action in that direction. On occasion, a scene intention will change, usually as a result of a major discovery or realization.

   Example: your character enters the scene with the intention of proposing marriage to another character, but after you enter, you discover your beloved kissing someone else. At that point, your immediate intention may change. Maybe you are now intent on leaving the room without being seen and embarrassed, or you are crushed and want to be alone to process this discovery, or perhaps your character now intends to take revenge on your rival!
   But most of the time your intention will stay the same, and only the tactics used to achieve it would change.

4. There is a dotted line that signifies a new tactic or attempt to change the line of action of the scene. Some of these changes (or transitions) are large and clear. Others are more subtle—the character is making a *slight* adjustment to get closer to the goal.

5. Note that obstacles often bring about immediate reactions in the characters. The character makes a discovery, recognizes it as an obstacle, and changes tactics. Realizations also bring about a change of tactics as the character reevaluates his or her own position in the circumstance.

In order to fully understand a scene, you might try this exercise: After you have done this for your character, shift gears and put yourself in the other character's position as you look at the same scene scored from the other point of view (that is, in light of the other character's intention). The same format applies, but the intention is different, so the tactics are different, the discoveries and realizations are different, and the obstacles are different!

Can you follow the line of action and thought process of the other character which support the changes?

One character's perception of what is happening in a scene is completely different from the other character's perception. That is why the scoring on the same scene will look entirely different, when scored from two completely independent points of view.

Also remember that every actor cast in these roles would bring different insights to the characters, bringing about even more possibilities of how this scene could be scored. It is that individual creativity combined with an actor's learned technique which makes the development of every role a unique quest.

SCORING YOUR OWN SCENE

Now, take the scene you have been assigned or pick one you would like to perform. After you have carefully read the whole play for storyline, style, and context, you are ready to score your scene. Use the scoring technique outlined in previous chapters as a model for your format.

1. Photocopy the scene so that you have lots of room to the left of the script text. You may wish to retype the scene in your computer so that you have a clear half-page to work on. Include your lines *and* those of the other character(s). Highlight your lines on the paper, if you wish.

2. Decide what your intention for the play is. You know by now that you will rework this several times, but you need to start somewhere, so write it in pencil. (Review Chapter Two on intention, which will help you make a good starting choice.)
3. Decide what your intention for the scene is. How does the action of this scene fit into the total play and your character's goal? Write the intention for the scene at the top of the page.
4. Now see what your character does to achieve that intention. Jot down the tactics you see as you read the scene. Notice the obstacles that pop up to interfere with the process toward the intention. (A review of Chapters Two and Four can help you with these decisions.)
5. Wherever you have a new tactic, mark it. Now check yourself. Go back, read the scene out loud, and see if you can sense the logic that leads to a change in tactic and if there is a corresponding change in the action. If you can, you did a good job! If not, go back to the tactic process. You might spend some time focusing on those places where you sensed a change and didn't notice a realization or tactical change. Find out what is happening to your character at that moment.
6. Where are the discoveries in the scene? What new information comes in through the senses? What do you see or hear (or taste or smell or touch) which affects your character's behavior? What effect do these discoveries have? (See Chapter Seven.)
7. Where are the realizations? How does your character process what goes on in terms of new understandings of the circumstances or situation? Does he figure out something important about himself? What is it? (See Chapter Seven.)

Understanding a clear notation system will help you find the fullest potential of your role. Keep on top of this process and make adjustments after every rehearsal. Make the system your own. You may eventually find that a journal, a chart, or a free-flowing schematic works better for you. But for now, master this standard approach to scoring the scene every time you work a role.

Tools to Help You

PHYSICAL TOOLS

When you act, you depend on many resources to do your job. Your own life experience is one of those resources, allowing those events in the scene that your character observes or takes part in to affect you. In other words, an actor will find the parallels with their own experiences. You try to connect the feelings and experiences of your character with your own, so that your work will be full and authentic.

But an actor has only three tools with which to communicate: their body, voice, and imagination. All of the character's mental, emotional, and experiential qualities must be expressed through you, the actor, using *your* body, *your* voice, and *your* imagination. Of course you say the things that the playwright has written—your lines. But your lines are only a part of what you have to communicate. Your body, too, reveals a lot about your character—especially about his true desires and emotional state.

As a well-trained actor, you get to choose what the audience learns about your character. These choices can tell them what your character is REALLY thinking, feeling, or wanting. What you say physically, with your body, may or may not correspond with what your character says verbally, using the playwright's words. Similarly, those words may or may not be confirmed by the way your character speaks—your tone of voice may say something different from the words. So you need to have control not only over your analytical processes and your feelings, but over your body and voice as well, so that you communicate exactly what you intend.

If your body and voice are not trained to be flexible and neutral, all of your characters will look and sound alike, no matter what differences you try to create. The audience pays to see a kind of transformation—a character brought to life through another human being, the actor. If that actor—you—carries indelible stamps of your personality through your own physical and vocal mannerisms, this transformation process cannot happen to its maximum potential; your character will not be fully realized or clearly transmitted to the audience.

You need to work hard to find the "neutral" you, in body and voice, so that you can communicate your character's intentions, obstacles, and tactics to the audience. This neutral you is not a zombie; you will still possess the same experiences and feelings and personality traits that you already have. The difference is that you will be able to make clear and supportive choices about your character, feeding this personality through the "neutral" you—without bringing all of your own baggage, particularly your physical and vocal mannerisms (regional dialects, poor enunciation, slouches, ways of walking, repetitive habits like tucking your hair behind your ears), to every role you play.

Finding Emotions in the Body

There is another reason to strive for neutrality: there is a natural (and strong) connection between your body and your emotions. Your body reveals who you are, what you want, and how you feel all the time.

If you want flexibility in casting, you need to know what your body is revealing about you to other people as they "read" your body language and posture. If you look like a discontented and closed person, you will be cast only in those roles. On the contrary, you may be happy and well-adjusted, but you habitually walk into a room looking down and caving in your chest, giving the impression that you are discontented and closed. If you look like a person who is out of shape and embarrassed about her body, you will be cast in those roles. On the contrary you may be in good shape but haven't yet developed an awareness of how your body allows you to relate to others in a positive way.

If you are in touch with the signals which your body sends to you and others, you will be able to make adjustments to more accurately portray and experience the life of each particular character. Each character will be different in the way they move and communicate physically. Your body is a tool for you to use in acting (and the rest of the time too!). Learn how it works, be able to fully utilize it and treat it well.

When you are happy, your body expresses exuberance and elation; when you are angry or sad, your body expresses those feelings. We are all used to this process. But it works in reverse too. What you do physically can induce strong emotions in you. In other words, what you DO can make you FEEL. Your body's behavioral signals can tell you what emotions you are feeling. Try the following exercise sequence to check this out.

1. Jump up and down, yelling "yah." Make fists and shake them as you jump. Keep going until you feel the blood pumping in your veins. What emotions do you feel? (Most likely you will start to feel angry or excited.) It's a physiological phenomenon. Your mind connects these physiological activities with potentially active or aggressive events in your life. That's the connection you make as the blood and adrenaline pump through your body.
2. Swing your arms loosely and whistle for a full minute. Sigh and smile. Take a stroll around the room, focusing on the physical sensations. Put a bounce in your walk. (You will probably begin to feel happy and at peace with the world.)
3. Slink down into a chair, stretch like a cat, and breathe out a "mmm." Shut out the world around you and revel in your own comfort. Move different body parts; explore the range of movement until each part is fully relaxed. (Most people feel sensuous when they do this.)
4. Focus on the ground and hold still. Let the breath drop out of your body whenever you need to let go of it. Feel the weight of your body and let yourself drop into the pull of gravity. Sigh deeply a few times, then gradually increase the depth of your breathing. How do you feel? Pretty low?

   (If you were to continue this breathing, increase the pace, and then hold your breath on an inhale and exhale on small high "huh" sounds, you would eventually feel like crying.)

These particular examples illustrate the inter-connection between body and emotion. Observe yourself as you experience the emotional ups and downs of daily life. What signals does your body send you as you run to get to class because you woke up late again? Observe other people; what can you tell about their emotional state from their body and movement? Come up with examples of your own.

Neutral Body

Chances are you have never really looked at yourself in the mirror in an objective way to see whether you are in proper alignment. Instead, you probably look in the mirror to see:

if your hair is okay;
if your underwear is showing;
if this outfit makes you look good or ugly;

if the colors go together;
if you're getting fatter or skinnier;
if you have any new zits;
etc.

But how often do you turn sideways to see if your shoulders, elbows, hip, back of the knee, and ball of the foot fall into a straight line? You should. Better yet, you should get a friend to check out this alignment so that they can add your ear to the top of this "plumb-line" list.

You should also make sure that your back and neck are long and extended. Too many of us walk around collapsed into our pelvic structure. Pulling your weight up and lengthening your spine and neck will keep you from letting all your weight go into the lower back. Using your stomach muscles, instead of letting your hips and back take the pressure, is also part of this realignment. (Good posture helps prevent back problems later on.) Work on this on a daily basis until it becomes natural for you.

Once you find the ideal neutral posture for your body, you can begin to play with variations on this posture. You will never be able to play a king or queen (or even a person in authority) if you cannot pull your own weight up. You can't play a disabled vet if you don't know how his disability affects his alignment.

It's not enough to have good alignment—although that is where you must start. You also need to build up your strength and stamina. If you are playing a character that has been beaten all his life, you will need to let your body reflect that fact. Unless you have control over your own muscles, you may find that playing this "down" role exhausts you. Or you may play a very athletic character that runs, climbs, gets into fights or wields a sword, and never stops moving during the course of the play. If you are not in shape, you will not be able to do several performances a week (including days in which you must do a matinee in the afternoon and an evening performance a few hours later).

If you are serious about being an actor, take a movement class for actors! Keep at it. Professional actors are very concerned with their physical health and development. You will find them in health clubs or dance studios or martial arts classes, working out and building strength, flexibility, and stamina so that they can play the largest variety of roles possible for their particular body types.

Remember: your body is one of your most important acting tools. Take care of it and train it. Proper physical training for an actor can and should take years. You must have the discipline to continue. We strongly suggest that you find a movement, dance, aerobic, martial arts, or yoga class and enroll. (It is impossible to include a full program of movement training in this chapter. In the meantime, however, there are a few physical exercises included in the appendix for you to try on your own.)

Observing Others to Build a Vocabulary of Your Own

There are lots of variations on alignment for characters with which you can experiment. Think about individuals you know who are "up" or "down." Do you know anyone who tends to lean forward most of the time? What types of people lead with their heads forward and their hips following? What types of people always look out of the corners of their eyes, never confronting you directly? Why do some people always cover their chests when they talk to you?

Walk around for a day or two looking at the ways people walk and sit and stand. Try to figure out why they move as they do. Can you tell anything about each one's personality, past training, interests, fears?

Observe also how people use objects. Watch someone take a drink in the middle of a story to recapture the memory more clearly before he passes it on to you. See how a cigarette smoker uses lighting up to flirt with the guy across the room. The way someone taps with a pen can reveal how he feels about the person he's talking to or how she feels about the topic under discussion. And there can be amazing and imaginative variations: if an actor peels a cucumber in such a way to terrify his scene partner and then makes rude gestures with it to throw the guy further off balance, it could be a delightful example of taking advantage of a prop to further the intention and reveal the inner life of the character. The ability to reveal the unexpected is a highly valued skill in actors.

Gestures can be a language of their own. Gestures can be overt, like a back-slap or pointing to something; or they can be covert, like a hand over the mouth to repress a word of anger or an inappropriate smile. A person may massage his head while he is trying to think of something, working the brain tissue to get the thoughts out. Or someone might stroke her arm to reassure herself when she's been emotionally hurt. Good actors choose gestures to support behavioral activity and reveal more about the inner life of the character. And they are in touch with their own bodies enough to let the body suggest expressions also!

Blocking

During your rehearsals, you will encounter the problem of when and how to move in your scene. If you've seen a play or a rehearsed scene, you have probably noticed that during the scene the characters may sit down, stand up, or move toward and away from each other. This stage movement is called "blocking." In a play, one of the director's main jobs is to block the play so that the movements of the characters reinforce what is happening in the scene. Sometimes the director will add "decorative" movement as well as movement that is pertinent to the intentional and emotional action of the scene. You can easily notice this decorative blocking in musicals, for example.

Full-length plays, as well as short scenes are blocked with relevant movement. If you figure out: 1. your character's intention, obstacles, tactics; 2. how she reacts to the partner; and 3. how to play these choices with truth and conviction, your scene will seem authentic to the audience. You must remember that as in life, a character moves for a reason. An actor must not wander all over the stage, but only move when the character is motivated, by a real need to move. If actors move erratically and without motivation, they have not really focused on intention or thought about how that intention translates into specific action.

Remember that movement often occurs when a character tries a new tactic, makes a discovery, or is momentarily overwhelmed by an obstacle. This basic rule will help you make intelligent and viable blocking and physical action choices.

Your script will probably tell you when to enter, sit, move to another character, etc. These are stage directions. Remember, however, that often these directions were not written by the playwright; often they are merely the notes taken by the stage manager to describe the director's blocking choices in the premiere production. Therefore, you usually have much more flexibility to determine the appropriate movement for your scene. (If you have a director, he or she may give you specific blocking. Then your job is to make that blocking work, to find realistic motivation.) When working a scene with a partner, try what's written to see if it works for you and is consistent with the dramatic action of the scene. If not, experiment a little on your own.

If you choose to do the script-required movement, you and your partner may still want to add movement to your scene that is not specified in the script. If you don't have a director to block the scene, you will have to figure out for yourselves how to do it; in other words, you will have to stage the action. First, figure out what movement is appropriate to the action and relationships of the scene, and then determine how best to execute it. Play around with this.

Move only when your character is motivated to move, in order to achieve an intention, or when a relationship changes. When you first put movement into a scene, move only at changes of tactics, or when relationships between the characters change. This will reinforce the action and relationships of the scene, and keep you from moving too much. If you depend upon whim or emotion to tell you where to move, instead of determining the relationships and power plays of the characters, you will end up with false, unmotivated movement. You will deny yourself the experience of the subtle ins-and-outs of physicality that actors use to reinforce our tactics. If you are playing your intention, obstacles, and tactics strongly, the audience will not be bored even if you never move out of your chair.

Good movements, which express the changing relationships throughout your scene, can be very few or very small. Bad movement choices (i.e., wandering, nervous gestures) will distract from your acting. Never add movement to a scene just for the sake of adding movement. Good movement choices will enhance your scene; bad choices will damage it.

We'll say it again:

Remember that movement usually occurs when someone tries a new tactic, makes a realization or discovery, or is momentarily overwhelmed by an obstacle.

The Use of Stillness

Don't think that you must continue to move every second that you are on stage, or in your scene. Stillness can be as effective as a movement or gesture. Stillness can convey that a character is stunned, emotionally overcome, or processing some particularly. If a character is giving a very important speech or crucial piece of information, it is best done with little movement. There is an important stage rule that applies here: *The eye will always follow movement, before the ear will process sound.* In other words, if there is movement anywhere on stage, the audience's eyes will focus on that movement first, and they may not really hear the important thing being said by another character. Movement distracts the eye, and the ear becomes a secondary function. So, if your partner is saying their most emotionally charged line, or a significant explanation, you should find a reason to be still. You can move again, if motivated, after that bit of dialogue is over, but give your partner full focus at these moments—and they should do the same for you.

Basic Staging Principles: Physical Relationships

Physical relationships between people reveal a great deal about their intentions, their fears/hopes, their emotional status, and their relationships. The best stage movement is movement that supports the relationships in the scene. Not only will the audience better understand the relationships and the dynamics of the changes in the relationship as the scene progresses, but also the actors will have a more immediate and truthful experience of the character's behavior. This all makes for a much better scene—well worth the time that it takes to block the scene carefully.

Here are some basic staging principles which will help you immensely in setting up the experience of the scene for the audience—and also for yourself.

1. First of all, experiment with your scene partner to find some obvious physical relationships. Remember to be responsible for your partner's physical safety during these exercises. In each of these exercises, take turns so each of you gets a chance to experience each type of movement.

    Leaning. With your partner, discover how many ways you can lean on each other. Do separate "leans" at first and then try to go from one "lean" to another without pausing. Don't be afraid to share your whole weight with the other person or to take responsibility for his or her weight. Leaning is reciprocal movement; it may express dependent or loving feelings.

    Pushing/Resisting. One of you pushes the other; the partner resists each push. Pushing is resistant; the partners are equally matched.

    Chasing. One of you chases the other to get something he or she needs. The partner rejects any advances by ignoring or leaving. Chasing reveals an unequal relationship or inability to communicate.

    Stalking. One sits in a chair or on the floor and the partner slowly stalks him or her, circling in from a great distance. Once the partner has arrived, he or she continues to circle around, exerting his or her physical presence over the other. Stalking represents a power play and one's attempt to gain mastery over the other.

Playing. This is a variation on "Swinging Statue," a game some of you may have played as children. One is "It" and swings the other gently in a circle by the hand and lets go so that the partner "flies away." The partner must then freeze in the position the momentum took him or her to. Playing expresses free spirits; and irresponsibility; the playing stops instantly when you freeze. (Tag or Red Rider are good alternatives.)

Molding. One of you molds the other into various shapes. The "mannequin" partner must maintain enough tension in all muscles (but continue to breathe) while this is going on to be able to sustain the position he or she is molded into. Molding and being molded are embodiments of manipulation and submission.

Leading. One of you is the leader and the other must follow wherever the leader goes, doing whatever the leader does. Leading involves agreed-upon dominance.

Leaving. One of you turns and walks away from the other. This may indicate rejection or abandonment. This is one of the most common and most powerful of the basic movements. There are lots of ways to accomplish this action, many of which affect the status of both actors deeply.

2. Discuss these experiences to see which of these reminded you of the basic relationship between the characters in your scene.

3. Determine the relationship dynamics of your characters in the scene. Transpose these dynamics into the basic action of the scene. Go over it with your partner, and decide the answers to the following questions:

    When are the characters "leaning" on each other?

    When does one "chase" the other?

    Does one character "push" or "pursue" the other? If so, what is the other character's response: resistance, denial, running away?

    Is there a direct or indirect "stalking" to gain power? Why does the partner "submit"?

    Do these characters trust one another enough to "play" with each other?

    Is it playing for real or does one of you have an agenda?

    Are the characters' relationships equal or does one "mold" and make the decisions for the other?

    Does one character "lead" another? If so, what causes the complete trust which the follower possesses? Does this dynamic last very long? (Probably not.)

    Does one character reject or abandon the other? What does the other character do as a result?

Putting the Scene into Its Environment

When you have figured out the physical relationships between the characters as they change throughout the scene, and explored ways to express these relationships physically, the next step is to decide where the scene takes place. The script gives you most of this information. Figure out the following things:

What kind of space is this? What is the purpose of this space? Is this a living room, a waiting room, a motel room, a porch, a clearing in the woods? What is the purpose of the room? If your scene takes place outside, adapt these questions to the outside space.

What do you absolutely need in this room? Don't put in anything you don't need to use during your scene.

Where are the doors and windows? Where does each door lead? What is the view from each window? Where is the nearest main road? Are there other pertinent buildings nearby?

What kind of furniture do you need to have in the room? How is it arranged? Is this a formal room or is this one in which the furniture moves to accommodate the immediate needs of the tenants? Is this a room which makes you want to burrow in and get comfortable, or is this a room which makes you want to get your business done and leave?

Who owns or lives in the room? What is your relationship to that person? Have you ever been here before? How many times? Do you like to come here? Or does this place make you uncomfortable?

The answers to these space questions become part of the given circumstances of your scene. They help define how your character will behave in the environment of the scene.

PRELIMINARY BLOCKING AND MOVEMENT EXPLORATIONS

At this point you should be able to do some preliminary blocking. You can start by literally leaning on each other, or chasing, or molding, or playing. After you put the literal relationships into the scene, you can find ways to suggest them without actually leaning or stalking or chasing. For instance, just moving closer to someone on a couch can feel to both characters like one is stalking the other.

Remember to include some moments of "leaning" in every scene; the characters would not remain there in the scene if they did not care about the other character or need the other character in some way.

Experience the physical relationships anew each time you rehearse. This is a side benefit to working this way: you can "feel" the character's situation and emotions much more clearly, and keep them fresh.

Continue to evaluate your blocking and physical actions in comparison to your intentions, obstacles, and tactics, too. Where are the changes? How does each change translate into the physical life of the character?

Try to find an appropriate place for stillness. How does that work? How is it motivated?

After you have run your scene with some blocking choices or explorations, debrief with your partner to see how these choices worked for the dramatic action of the scene.

SHARING THE SCENE WITH YOUR AUDIENCE

Your job is to create the scene as believably and clearly as possible for the audience, not just to experience it for the character (and for yourself). Once you have done some preliminary blocking and have made some decisions about your environment, it is time to consider the audience. If you make sure ahead of time that you are sharing the scene with them, you can perform the scene with your full concentration on what is going on inside the scene, without worrying about the audience at all.

It is important that most of the audience be able to see you and hear you most of the time. Is the audience going to be on one side, two sides, three sides, four sides, in a circle, or in a semi-circle around you? Once you know this, you can determine if the majority of people will be able to hear and see you during your scene. (If this is difficult for you to determine as you rehearse, get a class member to watch you and help you adapt your blocking for visibility and audibility.)

You also need to adapt the scale of your acting to the size of the room and distance from the audience. For example, a small movement (starting toward someone and stopping immediately) may have to be slightly larger and more energized for a large proscenium house. But that enlarged gesture would look phony and exaggerated in an intimate arena theatre.

STRONG AND WEAK MOVEMENTS

Audiences interpret some movements as strong and some as weak. Generally, the following formulations hold, but they are only general guidelines and only appropriate for a traditional proscenium theatre:

Walking toward the audience is powerful;
    walking away from the audience is weak.
Standing with your back to the audience is weak;
    facing the audience full front is strong.
The person who is higher has more power.
The person who is doing something different from everyone else has more power. (Two
    people sitting don't have the power of one person standing, especially if that person is
    closer to the audience.) A person who is facing away has more power than the one
    who is facing toward him (front to back position).
The person who moves more slowly, more quickly, more unevenly will
    take the focus from those who are more steady/ordinary.
The longer you and your scene partner stay in profile (facing each other, with
    the sides of your bodies toward the audience) while playing the scene,
    the weaker it becomes. Speaking to each other in profile can be used,
    but do not stay in that position for more than about 30 seconds! Find ways
    to adjust and vary your positions while speaking to each other.

Now go back and do some simple re-blocking of your scene, keeping these principles in mind. Remember to learn your blocking as thoroughly as you learn your lines. You don't want to think about where to move next; you want it to emerge naturally from the actions of the scene and the needs of the characters. Well-planned movement can strengthen your scene; unmotivated movement will weaken it. If you have questions about movement in your scene, check with your instructor.

PHYSICAL ACTION

Sometimes the script calls for you to do something specific, like drink a cup of tea, light a candle, sort laundry, or shove another character off a chair. You have to find ways to execute these "physical actions" so that they support the action of the scene, and so that the audience can see and hear what you are doing. In the case of any scripted "aggressive" or "fight" moves (like slapping, pushing, punching, etc.), always make sure that you have had adequate instruction in the safe ways to carry out these actions. These "physical actions" can be your best helpers in revealing the life of the character. If you think carefully and explore how and what they do, you will have a much clearer idea of why they do it.

Folding a T-shirt can reveal how you feel about its owner.
Wiping dishes can reveal how much you want to leave this place.
Turning the pages of a newspaper can reveal your interest in another person onstage.
Repeatedly smoothing your hair can reveal your insecurity.

For many actors, getting the right physical action can be the key to a truthful experience on stage. It has to be motivated and truthful movement, not just empty gesture. But when you make the right choices, they will fill in the gaps of the character's experience and help you to achieve her intention.

Remember Mike's Monologue? Here's what we would do to add the physical action choices to our scored script. PA = Physical Action.

Intention: to get Susan to call off the wedding

1.
Blocking: (Mike starts to leave and then comes back to Susan.)
T: to lay down the law
D: she isn't responding
O: her disbelief
PA: he stands firm before her

2.
T: to reassure her of his love without committing too much
O: his love for her
D: her hurt feelings
PA: he grabs her by the arms

3.
T: to get her to see how hard it is for him
O: she doesn't agree with him
R: it's getting close!
Blocking: he backs up a little
PA: he keeps her out of his space (puts up his hands in front of him)

4.
I'm not getting married! . . .

Blocking: one step towards her
5.
T: to bargain with her
O: lack of money
R: he doesn't want her to give up the ring he gave her
PA: he gets out his money from his pocket, takes off his watch, puts them on the table or holds them out to her

6.
T: to put the blame on a third party
D: she's beginning to hurt
R: he knows he's being a chump
O: weak argument
PA: picks up a magazine and waves it in her face

1.
I said, "I'm not getting married!" . . . I told you this would happen . . . I told you I wasn't ready. Do you remember? I said, "Susan, if I ask you to marry me, can I take it back if I want to?" And you said I could, didn't you? . . . Well, I'm taking it back now.

2.
I mean it's not that I don't love you, because I love you. I really love you, Susan, but it just can't be for keeps.

3.
I tried, Susan, I really tried, but it's getting close. There's only four days left. Just four more days and I can't go any further. . . . No, sir. No, ma'am. Uh–uh. No chance. No, siree. . . . Uh–uh. That's it. I can't do it. That's it!

4.
T: to plead with her for his freedom
D&O: that she isn't going to make this easy

5.
Look, I've got about twenty dollars on me. Here, take it as a deposit . . . and take my watch . . . and I want you to keep the ring. I know when a fella breaks up with a girl, he's supposed to get the ring back, but you can have the ring. That's fair, isn't it? I mean, another guy wouldn't do that, would he, Susan?

6.
Please stop looking at me like that. You shouldn't take it personally. It's nothing against you. It's the times we live in. India's overpopulated! We'll all be sterilized soon. The suicide rate is up. The air is polluted. Is that the kind of world you want to get married in? Is it, Susan? Is it?

7.

T: to paint Susan as the bad guy and himself as the victim
D: she is smiling at him!
R: he is going to have to get rough here
PA: gets in her face again, poking a finger at her nose
O: he knows she's no villain
Blocking: moves toward her and away alternating pattern two or three times

8.

Please don't make me marry you! I know this wedding is costing your parents a lot of money, but I'll pay back every penny of it.

PA: drops all gestures and attitudes and just looks at her
Blocking: When she does not answer, he slumps into a chair, defeated.

7.

I know what you're trying to do—make me look like the bad one. Well, it won't work. It won't work. Because I'm clean. I'm clean. You knew exactly what you were doing. You knew I was a confirmed bachelor. You knew I had trouble getting involved, but that didn't stop you. No, not you, baby. You decided to marry me and that was it. Well, who do you think you are, playing God with another person's life? Well, I have no pity for you. None whatsoever, because you're getting just what you deserve. So, get off my back. I owe you nothing, baby. Get it? I owe you nothing!

8.

T: to plead with her to postpone the wedding a while
D: her incredulous expression
O: his sense of fairness and love for her
R: he really wants to marry her

Give me a break. Take the pressure off me. Call the wedding off. Everything was going along great. We were having fun and smelling flowers. We could go on having fun for years. . . . And then some day maybe I'll have a lot of drinks and we could just sneak down to City Hall. That way I won't feel like I'm married. What do you say, Susan? Huh, Susan? What do you say?

You might have chosen different blocking or physical action choices if you had scored and worked this monologue. Each person works according to the logic of his or her own body and emotions. Experiment as you work your own monologues to see what actions will work best for you.

Other Physical Exercises

1. For whatever scene you are currently doing, add this as a rehearsal idea:

   a. Do a rehearsal based *only* on the blocking and physical action of the scene.

   That means do only the essential movement of the scene, the blocking and the physical action. Do not speak the words; if it helps, you can "speed-through" the dialogue silently in your head, but if you find that distracting, just do the movement. Concentrate on what is happening physically and intentionally, not verbally. A four-minute scene will take about two minutes to do if you do it with concentration on how the character's physical life informs the action of the scene. Don't rush the physical activity—use it carefully to inform you and your partner.

   b. Do it again and this time use a few words—just the minimum necessary to state your character's need. Make your physical life more important. Read the body language of your scene partner, or the other characters.

   c. Debrief and discuss what you discovered about the characters, about the action dynamics of the scene. Did you have any extraneous movement? Was there anything which you needed to add to clarify your action? Are there any physical habits which the character has had to develop to survive in this environment? Incorporate these insights into your character's physical life.

2. Observe the way people you know walk and move. Try to do what they do. Then figure out why they move as they do. Build a repertoire of information about how people move and how their movement reflects who they really are and what they really want.

VOCAL TOOLS

Neutral Voice

Everything we have said about the importance of training for physical neutrality applies to the voice, too. If you have ever listened to yourself on a tape recorder, you have had the ghastly experience of hearing how you really sound. This usually makes you say, "Oh, no! That can't be me! That's awwwwful!"

Our ears are undependable judges. We tend to hear what we want to hear or are used to hearing. Our ears fill in lots of missing sounds or allow for diphthongs that are not actually supposed to be in the words. If you grew up in Oklahoma, the deep south, upstate New York, or Northern California, then you pronounce words the way people in those regions do—this is called a "regional dialect." Most people are not aware that they have a regional dialect, unless they have had a voice and diction class.

Developing a neutral voice and a knowledge of the dialects or character variations that are possible opens up a world of possibilities for the actor. Instead of doing each role with your own regional accent, you can choose the neutral sound of Standard American Stage Speech, or pick up an appropriate dialect, or choose a specific vocal variation (like a lisp, nasality, low growls, etc.) for each character.

The actor begins with his or her own voice. You need to know that there are standard pronunciations for vowels and consonants. Vowels particularly lend themselves to regionalism; you should work on them for a standard American purity. If you come from the Southeast, chances are that you drop your tongue and extend the vowels. If you come from Brooklyn, your use of the lips adds a diphthong to the vowel sounds in "walk" and "your." In order to *fully* explore and learn about using your voice, you will need to take classes that focus solely on voice and diction. But we have included some important facts and general vocal exercises here.

Vocal exercises for vowels stress the proper lip placement and open-ness in the mouth. Good tone and vowel purity start from an open, yawning space in the mouth, not with a tight jaw. Since most of us tend to be lip-lazy and use the least possible energy when we speak, this feels strange at first. It soon becomes fun and a way of life. Command of vowels allows you to control and enhance your vocal tone (or melody).

Consonants are the articulators—the sounds that define the words. Adding clear consonants to your speech improves your ability to be understood. Some teachers focus on consonants as the percussive instruments of speech.

Consonants come in pairs, voiced and unvoiced.

Example: if you say a P and a B the same way, your speech will be difficult to understand. The fact is that your lips do different things when making these sounds. Try saying 'Buh - Puh' several times and notice what your mouth does on each consonant. Also, one is "voiced" and the other is not—this refers to the way air moves past your vocal cords, and whether you make a hard sound, or just let the air push or "pop" out of your lips. Other examples of paired vowels are G-K, S-Z, F-V, CH-SH, and D-G. In each of these pairs, your lips, tongue, teeth, or hard palate may play a role in the slight but important differences between the sounds. Try the "Guh-Kuh," "Sss-Zzz," "Fuh-Vuh," exercise with each pair—repeat the pair sounds several times until you identify how the apparatus of your mouth and the flow of your breath subtly changes for each sound. Figure out the specific differences, and that will help you enunciate each sound more clearly.

Because we tend to be lazy speakers, we often neglect to voice those consonants that should be voiced. Our lips and tongue do not work hard enough to make the sounds crisp and clear.

Example: If you were to say "hob-nob" in your usual style, chances are that you will say something closer to "hop-nop," because of a lack of mouth movement and tone in your consonants.

Problems such as these can be dealt with in a voice class or comprehensive study program. In the meantime, get hold of a good voice book or check out the exercises in Appendix B. The workings of the mouth and breath need to be strengthened just like your other physical muscles. If you are to be a skilled actor, you will need the discipline to develop your vocal and physical tools so that they help you, instead of hindering you.

Vocal Choices

In addition to the ability to make the voice neutral, so as to fit whatever vocal qualities specific character parts require, an actor must also be aware of the sort of vocal patterns and choices real people make in ordinary speech. Of course, all of us speak just fine for the community and region we live in, and when we talk to each other, our speech usually sounds normal and conversational.

Yet far too often beginning actors hear the critique: "Your lines just sounded memorized." But if you talked to this same beginner after a performance, he would not sound at all like he was speaking memorized lines, while chatting informally with you. What is going on? The actor has confused formal English with conversational speech while "acting."

Formal English is a written style; it involves the use of clear and carefully constructed sentences whose syntax and word choices all follow the rules of normal grammar and practice. A beginning actor may affect a stilted, unrealistic speech pattern, trying to speak "Formal English." Some even use an amateur (and incorrect) British accent, whether it is appropriate for the play/character or not! They believe that acting requires the kind of "Formal English" that is used in books and literature.

But this is rarely the language that *playwrights* use in writing *dialogue*. They construct informal, character-specific, conversational speech, which is inherently imprecise. They are allowed to utilize incorrect grammar, slang, and dialects to communicate the authentic personality, education (or lack thereof), social class, culture, and ethnicity of their characters. Each character in a play may have a different and individual speech pattern.

Conversational speech, as you might guess, is more informal and broken up than formal English. It uses more contractions, broken sentences, and short phrases. If the character is an upper-class, formal kind of person, or someone who uses precise phrasing, as in the case of a professor, or statesman, or nobleman, only then would the language in the play be as strict and correct as formal English. For example, many of George Bernard Shaw or Noel Coward's characters would speak in formal English. However, this sort of syntax is almost never used by playwrights such as David Mamet or Sam Shepard. Yet many beginning actors still try to impose formal dialogue on every character they play.

Playwrights struggle to create dialogue like people speak. But it is really up to the actor to be sensitive to the language the playwright uses, and to be aware of how people from different backgrounds actually sound. An actor must take the time to research, listen, and practice the speech pattern. They need to be aware of factors such as pace, rhythms, tonal variety, and diction.

Some Language and Vocal Exercises

1. **Formal/Precise vs. Conversational.** Practice each of the following lines, first as formal and precise language, then try to do them in a normal, conversational way. (Note how you change the pronunciation of words, especially articles of speech—a, the, an; and note also how your make words contract in the conversational mode, e.g., the formal "How are you?" becomes "How are ya?")

> I see a ball in the basket.
> How are you doing today?
> Where did you go today?
> Did you go to town?

The point here is not to get you to talk like backwoods moonshiners; however, you do need to learn how to do written dialogue as informal, conversational speech.

2. **Words as Sounds.** How do you indicate with words what are supposed to be sounds? Very often the playwright will use types of words and phrases to indicate that the character is making a kind of sound. Practice each of the following first by saying them as they are written, then do each by making the sound the words are actually intended to represent.

> Hurrumph! (a clearing of the throat)
> Hack, Hack. (a cough)
> Tsk, tsk. (a sound of disapproval)
> Gasp! (the sound of a gasp)
> Choke! (a choking sound)
> Yuck, Yuck, Yuck. (a laugh)

There are perhaps dozens of such idea words that playwrights use to indicate sounds. Learn to discover and perform the sound they indicate, *not* the words themselves.

3. **Vocal Patterns.** In conversational speech we normally do not speak in continuous, flowing sentences. We pause, stop, stammer, repeat, and use "place holders" such as "um," "uhh," or "like" as we go along. And so do most characters in most plays. Rarely does a character in modern drama go on and on, sentence after sentence without pauses, breaks, or interruptions. Even though sometimes the speech is written as a continuous paragraph, or monologue within the play, it is considered very weak and amateurish to perform it as one memorized and unbroken speech.

    a. **Filled Pauses** (pausing where you want meaning). Practice putting pauses into each of the following sentences. Justify your choices of pauses according to the lines spoken—that is, find reasons why the character would pause in saying each line.

    > I went into the house, and there on the table was the knife.
    > John is such a nice man, I mean, he is so good and so friendly.

You think I am a good person, but I need to tell you I am a bum.
Mom, I want to tell you what happened to the car, and I need to.
I don't know how to say this, but I can't, I just can't go along.

Remember that a **pause** is a moment where a character: is reacting to something; is busy thinking of the words they need to say; chooses *not* to say what they are thinking; or is trying to process something that just happened. A stage pause is **never** a passive moment of silence, with no thought going on. A pause is always "filled" with some kind of active thought that will communicate something specific to the audience.

Always work for conversational speech, not unbroken formal English.

b. **Breaks and Interruptions** (pausing where the playwright wants you to). This involves actually stopping—but as stated previously, it is not a passive moment. *Something* causes the character to stop: an overwhelming emotion; trying to find the right words to say something difficult; the knowledge that what you are about to say will be shocking; a hesitation to tell the truth, or a lie, or to hurt someone, etc. There can be many reasons, as long as they fit the purpose of the line. It often happens in very serious and dramatic moments, but sometimes the same kind of pause can be used in comic timing, as well. A good example of this is the legendary comedian Jack Benny, who was known for pausing and eloquently communicating a moment of irony or absurdity with his eyes, before continuing to speak. He could always get a laugh, just by doing that!

Playwrights often try to help the actor see these breaks by using ellipses (those little dots........) or slashes (————). Play each of the following sentences with breaks, but make choices to justify the breaks as believable conversational speech.

I went to his side and he........died.....in my arms.
The box opened and.....there was nothing........it was empty.
She said that I was no good-----I was not her type.
You can't mean that you......don't love me?
He went to kiss her......and fell off the porch.
And then the dog.....ate....her hamster.

c. **Stammers and Repeats.** This is a very common element in a lot of dialogue, and the playwright uses punctuation to show you what to do. Rehearse and play the stammers and repeats in each of the following as real conversational speech, with clear justifications for why your character would be stammering and repeating.

So you . . . um . . . you think it's OK . . . it's OK to just dump me?
Who do you think . . . who do you . . . who do you think I am?
And then he said . . . he said . . . well, he said, "You won it all!"
I went down there and . . . and . . . and they all laughed at me.
So he, like . . . like yelled . . . "Hey, do you like want to . . . go to the dance?
I . . . um . . . uh . . . wanted to say . . . um, say that . . . you look nice today.

One stage rule regarding repeats: If you say the same words/phrases two or three times each time you say it, it must be somewhat different. This can be accomplished with pace, volume, or emphasis. Often a playwright will use capital letters to indicate where emphasis should be placed or volume raised. Try some examples of this:

"What do you mean? I said, WHAT do you mean?......WHAT... DO... YOU... MEAN?"
"Oh, my...IS that a.....? Is THAT a.....? Is that a really HUGE .....moosehead??"
"He dumped it here....he just DUMPED it here...he just dumped it!........Right HERE!"
"Mary took it upstairs.....she TOOK it....upstairs. MARY took it!"

A warning: The purpose of these vocal exercises is to make you aware of some of the ways in which normal speakers of conversational English break up the written words into the natural flow of real conversations. DO NOT attempt to apply broken, pause-ridden phrasing and stammering speech to every character, or every script. Look carefully for cues from the playwright, and be judicious in your use of these vocal techniques.

These techniques can help you deliver lines naturally, like someone really speaking normal conversation; or they can be overdone and end up making you seem like a very strange and speech impaired character. Too much variation from regular tempos and patterns of speech can slow down the momentum of the scene, cause the energy to die and make you appear to be "trying too hard." A few specific, interesting, and motivated vocal choices can add interest and meaning to a scene.

It is always useful to explore and try different things with line delivery, that's how you make discoveries! But you need to use good sense about what sounds right, or appropriate. If you are not sure, ask an instructor to help you with your choices.

CHAPTER TEN EXERCISES

There are physical and vocal warm-ups in Appendix D which will give you a start in trying out the techniques discussed here.

Chapter 11

Additional Techniques and Creativity

By now you understand many of the fundamentals of acting included in this class, and have mastered some of the basic skills, so it is worth considering some of those elements in more detail. Of course, one class will not substitute for the years of training in all of the performance areas necessary for superior acting; but it is useful near the end of the course to explore some of the basic principles in more detail. If you choose to continue your study in this art, you will need to have some idea of the next steps.

By now, you have likely seen a lot of performances in class and done several scenes yourself. It should be clear to you that acting is both a lot more work, and a lot less frightening than you might have imagined. The amount of time and critical judgments that go into the lengthy rehearsal process is quite a bit more than most non-actors realize. No one can do a believable performance by just memorizing lines and hoping for the best.

But it is also a lot less strain for many actors, because once you have a specific technique that you can rely on, have done the "head work" of analysis in early rehearsals, and have discovered the depth that focused movement and voice work can add to a performance, bringing a character to life can be a soaring and freeing experience. You have done your preparatory work. Now, in front of an audience, it can all come together with ease and joy.

Certainly there are a series of tasks the actor must work through prior to performance, as we have outlined throughout this text. Some tasks are more difficult than others, but all require effort and thought. It is exactly like learning to sing or sail, play a guitar, hang-glide or surf—you must learn the basics, put time and effort into practicing, learn from your mistakes and slowly gain confidence—but the sense of accomplishment and exhilaration, when you *know* you've done it well, can be immensely satisfying.

If you are able to put advocacy, commitment, and energy into your role, you will create a fully-rounded character—with recognizable behavior, authentic needs, invested with emotional truth, and a stake in the importance of achieving his or her goals—with whom your audience can identify, and by whom they can be moved. It is in this connection with the audience—*moving* them, and ultimately validating their own human experience—that you can find your gratification as an actor—that electrifying moment when you, through your performance, are able to change hearts and minds.

ACTIVE LISTENING

Throughout this text we have been stressing the importance of listening to the other character on stage with you. Without listening there is no believable acting. If you pretend to listen, the audience can spot it every time. But what are you supposed to listen to?

Consider why characters talk and listen in the first place. They are in a world where their intentions drive them; they are, at every moment, trying to achieve something. Thus, they never talk unless they are trying to get what they want most. Everything they say is connected to achieving their goals, their intentions. They do not waste words.

And why do they listen to each other? Because they are trying, always, to hear if their own actions, their own tactics, are helping them achieve their intentions. Most frequently this listening involves trying to hear three separate but closely related things:

1. Is the obstacle, the resistance the other character represents, lessening because of what I am doing and saying?
2. Is what the other person is doing and saying helping me toward the desired intention I want to achieve? Or are they creating new obstacles?
3. Is there new information, or new tactics that I can use here to make it easier for me to achieve my intention?

This is **active listening.** Passive listening is just standing there as an actor waiting to hear the cue words which let you know it is your turn to speak again. *Active listening is thinking as the character and listening for clues from the other character about how you are doing and how you need to change or modify your tactics to succeed.*

Recall that the character you play does not know what the other person is going to say next, but your character is very focused to learn what it is. In fact, it might be helpful to think of active listening as the difference between two points of view:

a. What you hope the other person will say when you are done talking, and
b. What that person actually does say.

The more A and B are alike, the closer you are to your intention. The more difference there is between A and B, the more you need to alter what you are doing to get the other person to say what you want. Active listening lies in knowing what you want the other person to say, and then comparing that with what they actually do say.

Let's look at an example. You go home for Thanksgiving, and when your mother comes home from work, you ask her if you can have $40.00 to go buy a new backpack. Your intention is to get the money and buy the backpack. Let's start with what you **hope** your mother will say:

You: Hi, Mom. Can I have $40.00 to go buy a new backpack?
Mom: Why sure. I noticed your old one was pretty worn out.

OK. That is what you **hoped** for. But listen to what she **actually does say:**

You: Hi, Mom. Can I have $40.00 to go buy a new backpack?
Mom: Are you out of your mind? You already HAVE a decent backpack. You think I'm made out of money?

Now, what are you going to say next? And what do you have to do if you are going to stick with your intention? Perhaps you are going to try to reason with her, or beg and whine a little.

You: Gee, Mom. I really need a new backpack. I can't fit all my books in this one and the seams are splitting. And I promise I won't ask for any more money. Pleeeasse?

But whether you beg or not, if this were a real event in your life, you would be listening like crazy to learn what your mother would say. And once she spoke, you would then make decisions about how to respond and react. That is active listening.

Active listening always includes that drive to see how you are doing, to learn what the other person is going to do, and to react to the difference between what you hope they will say and what they actually say.

Of course, this all ties into reaction techniques.

REACTION ANALYSIS

It has been said by more than one famous teacher of acting that "Acting is simply good reacting." Surely you have seen some acting scenes where the characters were not reacting sufficiently to each other. Perhaps critiques you have received on your own performances have included the note: "React more! We can't tell how your character feels about this!" But what is good reacting? How does it work?

In real life you are constantly reacting to things around you. Some things are hardly worth noticing, like blocking out the tick of the clock in your room. Other reactions can be large and life threatening, like jumping back on the curb to avoid the car running the red light as you were entering the cross walk. Some reactions are almost entirely automatic: a loud noise makes your eyes blink; a book falling off the top shelf makes you raise your hands over your head. But many of your reactions center on what people around you are doing, especially when they are doing something that does or might have an impact on what you are trying to do.

In plays, that latter kind of reaction is most needed, and most commonly ignored by the novice actor. Even the weakest actor knows enough to jump when a gun is suddenly fired on stage or knows to drop dead after the secret poison has been drunk. But the reactions required in response to what other characters are doing is often more subtle. Let's look at the process in more detail.

Anatomy of a Reaction

Except for automatic reactions, like ducking when a tree branch falls or holding your breath when you go under water, all reactions in people—and in characters on stage—are the result of something happening, and a quick series of separate mental steps. Here are the steps our mind goes through when we have a reaction:

1. We *recognize* a change;
2. We *evaluate* the change in relation to our own intention;
3. We *select* a way to respond in relation to the change (a tactic);
4. We *act out* a response to the change.

Consider an example: You are a new student on campus and standing at a street corner trying to figure out where the library is. A stranger—a 60-year-old man in shabby clothes—comes up next to you and stops. You then go through the four steps:

1. You recognize he has stopped next to you.
2. You evaluate that he could be a dangerous pervert, or a poorly dressed professor, or just an old guy standing on the corner next to you.
3. You select a tactical response: pretending he is not even there, or moving away from him, or asking him where the library is.
4. You act out a response: by moving away from him.

Each step in the process takes time. The amount of time depends on the size of the change, its potential impact on the character, and the character's ability to come up with an appropriate response to the change. If the shabby looking man had a gun in his hand, it would have taken the lost student only a split second to go through the four steps: "the guy is dangerous, I'm out of here!" But, if the man had started a conversation about, say, "the rigors of academic life in the modern university," the new student would have much more difficulty (and would need more time) to decide what to do and say next.

In this case the steps of the reaction would take more time because the choices would be more complex, and the student would probably be unsure as to how to respond to this intellectual conversation.

Reactions always take time. Sure, the next lines in the script are right there, but in creating the character, the actor must take the time to allow the *character* to decide what to do or say next, not merely go right on saying memorized lines.

Remember: There is not a hard and fast rule which determines how much time it takes for a character to react—it depends on the character, the character's ability to think and come up with alternate responses, and the possible new actions available within the given circumstances of the play. But characters rarely rush reactions; only weak actors do.

Don't rush it. Reacting requires thinking. You, the actor, know the next line to say, but the character you are playing does not; your character needs time to react to what the other person has just said before deciding what to say and do next. Each time you say a line in a play, it should sound like you are saying it for the first time—that you just now thought of these words in reaction to what the other character has said to you.

Remember the four steps in that reaction: recognize, evaluate, select, act out.

Another commonly used term for this is "listen, absorb, speak." It is during the "absorb" part that you will use the first three steps of reaction in order to process what you heard, before you act out or "speak."

CREATIVITY IN ACTING

A beginning actor who reads this whole text carefully will notice what looks like a contradiction between some of the advice on analysis and performance. In almost every chapter the intellectual aspects of acting are stressed: the need to study the character, the importance of doing careful analysis, the necessity of reading the scene and the play over and over, the importance of carefully scoring the text. But then, often in the same paragraphs stressing critical details, you are also encouraged to do artistic things like: "Make dramatic choices! Go for it! Be in the moment! Put yourself in the scene!" So, what's it going to be: think or feel?

The easy answer, of course, is to say you must do both to succeed. And that *is* good advice. However, it is important to point out that the best character analysis in the world is really only a tool to use on the way to performance. You truly must be creative to bring your assigned character to life in a way that is at once believable, moving, and truthful for your audience.

In a real sense, to succeed as an actor you must go beyond your analysis work. Yes, the critical exploration of intellectual investigation defines a lot about who your character is. But unless you can incorporate all that analysis into your body, into your emotions, feelings, and physical self, very little is going to happen to the audience watching your efforts. And that is where the creative process must come in.

Creative Muscle Memory

In earlier chapters we pointed out how much of acting is like a skill in sports, something that requires a lot of practice and repetition to be mastered. In fact, part of that skill has to be discovered and learned anew with each role you play. For every character you play, you must train yourself to use all parts of yourself in the same way the character would: your voice, your body, gestures, movement, response time, mannerisms, thinking process—all need to be trained and adjusted to fit each specific character.

Muscle memory—the process of training your body to react in the physical and emotional ways the character does—is an important tool in the creativity of becoming a character. Here are some examples of how you have already used muscle memory in your own life: do you remember when you were first learning to drive and all the things you had to do felt foreign and difficult to remember? But in a short while, it became automatic, and you could confidently drive the car without trying to remember each move. This is your muscle memory kicking in; the same concept applies to learning to ride a bicycle, water ski, ice skate, play tennis, etc. At a certain point, your muscles just know what to do and do it, without you having to focus on your balance and movements so much.

When you are acting, it is the product of rehearsing all those mental and physical parts to work like the character would. You will need to adjust your voice, your body, gestures, movement, response time, mannerisms, and thinking processes to those of the character. The results are that, with a lot of rehearsal, you will no longer have to "think" about how to move or react or speak as the character—you will have made all this a part of your body, and you will be free to act the character.

While in the rehearsal process, you must be creative. You must become a risk taker. You must allow yourself to explore the physical and emotional range of possibilities that your character might attempt. Certainly, your mental analysis and homework have defined the range of possibilities for your character as well as made clear the kind of world in which the character lives. But you must experiment with what you do as the character. You must be creative, inventive, and free in rehearsal to explore different ways to speak, move, think, and react. You need to explore and try different variations of the amount of time you use for your character to think, speak, and react; you must explore and experiment with the use of movement, your relationship to the furniture, and your physical relationship to the other character in the scene. You will find some things don't work at all, but some will feel right, and strengthen your character. These different options will help you discover how to get your body, mind, and emotions into a match with the character's.

In short, the rehearsal process is a time of creative invention. Remember: Acting is not like a math class where there is a right answer. Acting is the celebration of many answers, of many different ways to create a character. You must search and explore to find good choices.

Muscle memory is a great part of the actor's repertoire: it locks much of the character into your body so that it will automatically and naturally come out when you go on stage. But, if you are not creative and responsive in rehearsal, the only thing your muscle memory is going to store is the same old drab, boring, and self-conscious uncertainty that you began rehearsals with, or worse—all of *your own* movement, gestures, mannerisms, ways of speaking and reactions, rather than the character's. What you rehearse is what you store in muscle memory, and that is what you get in performance. And if you do not use that rehearsal time well, it will be apparent to the audience. The quality of your performance comes directly from the quality of your work in rehearsal.

Creative Responsiveness

There is another very important creative skill involved in acting which you must strive to perfect. That is the skill of responding to the other character. All the exercises about reaction, given circumstances, scoring, and everything else related to acting are lost if you do not allow yourself to learn to develop creative responsiveness in the rehearsal and performance process.

This kind of responsiveness is both a state of mind and a skill to master. **Creative responsiveness** means being open and willing to build and adjust your own responses as an actor, based upon the performance that is coming from the other actor in the scene you are rehearsing or performing. It requires that you be alert and aware, which is a concept we worked on earlier—being "in the moment." This means living each section of the scene, each line of dialogue, as though you do not know what is going to happen next.

Creative responsiveness takes you beyond that; it involves allowing your resourceful and creative self, your inventive and imaginative side to come out in the rehearsal (and in the performance). You need to almost forget what you know about the character, stop thinking about rehearsal, and instead act on your intuition and responses; respond to what the other actor is doing as the other character in your scene. If there is a subtle change in the delivery or emphasis or sound of a line from the other character, you need to respond to *that*, not just deliver your line exactly as you did in rehearsal. This can lead to really interesting development in the character's relationship.

When you and your partner both move into creative responsiveness, interesting, surprising, and truly dramatic things begin to happen to your scene. The characters clash, tension and energy begin to build. Subtle feelings can rise to the surface, making a love scene more believably emotional. This is how interesting dramatic choices really take shape. Here is where you allow yourself to try lots of different approaches, and go with the energy of the scene as you and your partner develop it.

You have to practice this, just like any other skill. Though it may at first seem like a strictly emotional thing to do, this is really a technique to master. It is hard at first to let yourself just respond; years of cultural training, social conditioning, and even self consciousness interfere with this technique. Your first instinct may be to stay "safe" and do exactly what you have learned intellectually about your character.

In using this tool, in learning to work with and respond creatively to your partner, on a deeper lever, you begin to discover more about the drama and the internal life of your character. The relationship will continue to develop through the active use of your imagination, instincts, intuition, and creativity more than you could ever find through intellectual exercises alone. But this is a fairly advanced step, and you must master the basics before progressing into true creative responsiveness.

WRAPPING IT ALL UP

Well, here we are at the end of the text. By now you have the tools you need to do the job of acting. You have a technique (intentions, obstacles, tactics), a methodology (the rehearsal process), a grasp of scenic structure (builds and moments), a healthy understanding of the pitfalls (stage fright), and appreciation for the work of other actors (partners and critiques), and some goals (neutral body, voice, creative responsiveness). You even have schedules and forms that will take you through the roles you develop (character analysis sheets, acting critique).

This is just the beginning. These basics will serve you well as you advance in your craft, but you will also discover much more as you grow and learn. It takes a certain amount of life experience to act. As you gain that life experience, you will have much more to contribute to your roles. The great actor Sir Laurence Olivier believes that he did not do justice to the role of King Lear until he played it in his 70s. By that time, he felt that he had sufficient life experience (himself, as a person, not just as an actor) to understand, play, and truthfully advocate Shakespeare's tragic king. Acting is one field in which, if you stay open and honest and teachable, you will only get better and better as you mature. And there is no "end" . . . there are always more things to learn about a character, which is why you can play the same role again later in your life and you will have new insights and a fresher approach than the last time you played the character.

Think of it this way: You are now ready to embark on a series of explorations. Life is your school. Take advantage of all it has to offer you. Keep your eyes open and learn from your successes and failures and from those around you. You will be surprised at how much you learn about the characters you play.

As you learn more about life, you have more to offer when you are cast in a play. Look at each character as a chance to find out more about the human condition. See each role as an opportunity to understand people better. Give each part as much of yourself as you can find to give. The rewards will take you far beyond the applause of closing night.

Espresso Bar

Kristin McKague[1]

(A coffee house in San Francisco. JESSICA enters, goes to espresso bar, orders.)

JESSICA

An espresso, please—

ALAN

(Enters. Over her shoulder to bar attendant.) No steamed milk, but how about some cream? On the side?

JESSICA

Alan! Hello! *(Hesitates a minute, then embraces him. To attendant.)* Yes, cream, please. In a little . . . on the side. Thank you.

ALAN

When did you get back?

JESSICA

About a week ago. How are you?

ALAN

Fine . . . Good.

JESSICA

Good.

ALAN

And you?

JESSICA

Great.

---

[1]*Espresso Bar,* by Kristin McKague. Reprinted by permission of the author.

ALAN

Good.

JESSICA

I called you.

ALAN

Yeah?

JESSICA

Yeah.

ALAN

Oh, right. Gordy took the call.

JESSICA

I wasn't sure if I'd even remembered the right number.

ALAN

You weren't gone that long.

JESSICA

It sure felt like a long time—

ALAN

Long enough to forget.

JESSICA

I just felt pretty far away, is all. *(Her espresso is up.)* Oh, thank you. Well, I'm sitting over there . . . working.

ALAN

I'm with some people.

JESSICA

Right.

ALAN

Don't forget your cream. On the side.

JESSICA

Thanks . . . Who'd you say you were with?

ALAN

I'm meeting . . . umm . . . I'm meeting Maude here.

JESSICA

Maude?

ALAN

Yeah.

JESSICA

Oh. So, how's Gordy?

ALAN

We haven't seen much of one another.

JESSICA

But you two were so close.

ALAN

Well, now Maude and I are close.

JESSICA

Oh, good. *(Laughs.)* Wrong of me to ask.

ALAN

Maude and I are pretty intimate.

JESSICA

Shit.

ALAN

I wrote to you.

JESSICA

You did?

ALAN

Yeah. But I never mailed it. I hate writing letters, you know . . .

JESSICA

Yeah.

ALAN

That's your thing.

JESSICA

Well, it's a side line . . .

ALAN

No, that's your thing. Life is your side line. *(To attendant.)* Could I have a mocha, please? I'd like that with whipped cream and slivered almonds and enough honey so that it drips down the side of the coffee mug. Thank you. Maude turned me on to that one.

JESSICA

No.

ALAN

(calls) MAUDE! OVER HERE! *(He waves.)* Be seeing you, Jessica.

JESSICA

See you. Say hello to Maude for me.

ALAN

I will *(Exits.)*

JESSICA

(To attendant.) Skip the cream. I'll drink it black.

"Blonds" by Jon Jory[1]

CHARACTERS

SUSAN   MARTY

SCENE: *SUSAN sits on a bench on a college campus on a sunny morning. She is reading. MARTY enters. He is wearing a running suit.*

MARTY

Hi. (SUSAN glances up but doesn't respond.) Incredible day, huh? (No response.) You don't happen to know what time it is, do you?

SUSAN

No, I don't know what time it is. Furthermore, you don't care what time it is. You are bugging me because I am blonde, reasonably attractive, and sitting here alone. Know what that makes the score for today? Eight. And it's like ten A.M. A guy jogged by a minute ago and says, "Great legs." I ignore him. He jogs around the bench saying, "Great hair," "Great eyes," "Great tennies." I read. He stops, pulls my paper down with his forefinger, stares into my eyes and then calls me a tease and runs off. Fun, huh? Coming down from the dorm this old geezer in a walker beckons me over. I think he needs help. I go. He wants to know do I get off on older men. I pick up the campus paper, this guy buying *Hustler* thinks it's a coincidence we can both read. Would I read with him over a cup of coffee at the Student Union? I say I've already had my coffee and he asks if, in that case, I'd like to go fool around in his apartment. I have been whistled at, leered at and propositioned and Monday is just starting. It's like this seven days a week, and is it flattering? No. Is it titillating? *no.* It is a colossal, horrendous, never-ending, incredible hassle. Now, in the words of my back-water Baptist eighty-six-year-old grannie, "Finish yer grits an' git."

MARTY

Your day and my day have not been exactly the same. I have not been whistled at or propositioned. I look so vulnerable that when I stop at a corner people try to help me across the street. I have passed many attractive women on this campus who are more interested in litter than in me. If, from a beautiful girl, I got vibrations other than *get lost* or *cease to exist*, I would assume I had wandered into a Walt Disney movie. My native sexuality has been eroded, erased, eradicated until I am

---

practically asexual. I have had three dates in the last six months and two of them were friends of my mother's supervisor at the I.R.S. Tax Audit Division. One was passable despite the fact that acne obscured her natural graces, and the other two had obviously been made examples of by an old-testament and unforgiving God. Why are you bugging me?

SUSAN

On the other hand, why are you bothering me?

MARTY

I wanted, God forgive me, to know what time it is. So that my dotty mother would not, perish the thought, have to hold breakfast for me.

SUSAN

You didn't choose to ask me because I was blonde, conveniently alone and, for you, doubtless a fantasy object?

MARTY

I chose to ask you because you are the first person I saw when the question arose, because it seemed unlikely you would mug me, and because you happen to have on a watch.

SUSAN

It is eight fifty-three.

MARTY

Allah will bless you and your camel. *(He starts to walk off)* You know, you really piss me off. Begging your pardon. I happen to be an intelligent, relatively entertaining, more than moderately sensitive, intensely loyal, surprisingly curious, amazingly supportive, non-chauvinist, and though I know I don't look it, a physical education major. But it would never occur to you that I could be considered as a companion, confidant, lover or husband to your royal, protestant-princess, unattainable self. You are so buy being annoyed by what you take to be sexual compulsion and male generalization that you wouldn't recognize a decent, caring man if he walked up and spit in your eye.

SUSAN

This has the virtue of at least being an entertaining line. On the other hand, you are not favoring me with your resume because you want friendship or regard. You are hoping in a perverse way that this nuthatch conversation is going to end up getting me into the sack.

MARTY

I have yet to construct the conversation that will end up in my getting anybody in the sack. I am a twenty-two year old virgin graduate student without significant prospects. Now whattaya wanna do about it?

SUSAN

We could be talking politics, we could be talking philosophy, we could be sharing the territorial imperatives of llamas or discussing heavy subatomic particles in the nuclei of atoms, but no, we are once again pounding out the tribal rhythms of the boring old mating dance. I hate being a sex object and you hate being a virgin, but we are incapable of doing anything but looking each other over.

MARTY

You are looking me over?

SUSAN

No . . . Well, maybe, in a sort of abstract sociobiological manner.

MARTY

Lady, I live off crumbs. You could be overflying me in a Russian U2 and I would be grateful for the glance.

SUSAN

Look, think of me as a rock or a Carolina sand pine, okay? *(She goes back to her reading.)*

MARTY

Listen, lemme suggest a deal. I will outline for you here a three-date package. First, a dinner and a movie. I pick the restaurant, pizza declared off limits, you pick the flick. This allows conversation without too heavy an emphasis on personal sharing. Next, a day with the university's permanent art collection at Wilder Nail where we can read our personal preoccupations into non-objective art, and finally an evening at a friend's spend in conversation and three- or four-way relating. During the aforementioned date package, there will be no touching or libidinous innuendo of any kind, and the entire package can be extended or terminated by mutual consent during free-form negotiation subsequent to the above meetings.

SUSAN

You're a lawyer, right?

MARTY

No, I am not a lawyer. I am probably the only person you have met this week who aspires to be a major league baseball scout.

SUSAN

What is your full name?

MARTY

Martin "Fork Finger Fastball" Abromowitz. The middle name I picked out for myself.

SUSAN

Pleased to meet you, Fork Finger. I am Susan Wright.

MARTY

You have met Mr. Abromowitz and I have met Miss Wright.

SUSAN

This is a dumb joke.

MARTY

Enter it in the con column.

SUSAN

All right, Mr. Abromowitz, I accept your proposal. There is to be no sexual content. No compliments. No inquiry into previous male-female relationships. No touching. No longing looks. No hustle. And in your case, most importantly, no bad jokes.

MARTY

Ordinarily, I would prepare a contract, but in your case I will accept a handshake as a tender of good faith. *(They shake hands.)*

SUSAN

I will meet you at six-thirty in the women's lounge of the Susan B. Anthony Dormitory Complex, Building B. Dress casual.

MARTY

An interesting point is that this very possibly is a landmark boy-meets-girl situation. Relating contracts at the beginning of what used to be called a, shhh, don't let anybody hear this, *flirtation,* could possibly transform Western civilization as we know it.

SUSAN

I don't doubt that for a minute, Fork Finger, but you know what it makes me wonder? *(A pause.)* Whether you'll light up right after the first time we do it?

(BLACKOUT)

More on the Tools and How to Use Them

Here are some additional exercises that you can work on to help you begin to achieve neutrality and flexibility in your body and voice—essential tools for the serious acting student.

NEUTRAL BODY

Let's spend some time on you—getting you into a neutral physical alignment. You will find this process to be eye-opening, yet relaxing. Then comes the constant vigilance, which can take the rest of your life to ensure that this "new you" becomes the "real" you, the neutral base from which you approach all your acting.

Floor Alignment

1. The class counts off by 1's and 2's; then each of you chooses a partner of the opposite number who is about the same height and weight as you are. The whole class does the first part of this exercise together as the teacher verbally instructs them; you will work with your partner later in this session.

2. Follow these directions as specifically as possible, always concentrating on your breathing, and trying to relax your whole body:
   a. Lie on the floor on your back with your knees up and arms down by your sides.
   b. Try to feel the surface of the floor on your whole back, keeping the small of the back relaxed into the floor as much as possible. Let your legs relax out or lean against each other at the knees.
   c. Concentrate on your breathing as you continue with these instructions.
   d. Try to lengthen the back of your neck to elongate the spine and stretch your torso to its maximum height.
   Gently roll your head from side to side, feeling the weight of the head as it falls gently to each side and is lifted up again in order to roll to the other side.
   e. Now gently pick up one hand and let it fall to the floor again.
   f. Do the same with the other hand. Rock the legs in the hip sockets for a few seconds and then stretch the legs out so that they are fully extended.

3. The 1's remain on the floor and the 2's stand at the feet of their partners. The 1's should continue to concentrate on their breathing and try to perceive the adjustments that are being made to their alignment. The 2's will follow the teacher's directions, always being careful to handle their partners' bodies gently and with firm/sure control.

   a. Instructions to the 2's: Pick up the heels of your partner and gently pull toward you, leaning away with your whole body as you pull. Set the heels down carefully. Now go up to your partner's head and gently lift the head from the base of the skull, supporting the weight with both hands. Again, pull gently away from the body and set the head down carefully.

   b. Repeat the heels and the head, keeping the vertical line of the body clearly in sight; this is your chance to realign the shoulders over the hips over the knees over the heels and to position the head over them all. You may also adjust the arms if necessary. Try for perfect symmetry. Remember to leave the body with the head pulled away from the torso. Your partner should feel as if he or she is suspended from a rope from the back of his or her head.

4. Once the 2's have made their final adjustments and the 1's have had a chance to absorb this placement, it is time to reverse and give the 2's a chance to experience this marvelous feeling.

5. After everyone has had a chance to be gently stretched and aligned by a partner, it's time to stand up. Instead of leaping up and destroying the work you have just done, get to your feet carefully, by rolling up to a standing position:

   a. Slowly sit up and, leaning over, get your feet under you, so that you dangle from the hips like a puppet whose upper strings have been cut. Roll up to a standing position, one vertebrae coming into alignment at a time. The head should come up last.

Standing Alignment

1. Standing alignment from the side in pairs.
   The 2's will be the first subjects this time.

   a. If you're a 2, stand as straight as you can, focus your eyes ahead and concentrate on your breathing.

   b. If you're a 1, step away from your partner a couple of steps to the side, just enough to be able to see your partner's whole body in profile. From this vantage point, check to see if the following points of the body are directly in a line perpendicular to the floor: ear, shoulder, hip mid-point, knee, ball of the foot. If they are not, gently re-align your partner to bring these into position. Take a minute to give your partner a chance to absorb this sensation of perfect alignment.

   c. Now reverse the process and give the 1's a chance to find out where their proper alignment is.

   d. Some trouble spots to watch out for:
   > lower back curved in and stomach muscles out;
   > rigid shoulders pulled back;
   > head and neck forward;
   > locked knees;
   > weight of whole body on heels.

2. Standing alignment from the front in pairs.
   Start with the 2's again.

   a. If you're a 2, take your aligned position.

   b. If you're a 1, step away to the front of your partner. This time look at your partner's whole body in terms of lines that are parallel to the floor. Are the shoulders dropped and level?

Are the hip-bones parallel to the floor? (If you can't see the hip-bones, ask your partner to show you where they are.) Do some manual realigning and give your partner a chance to absorb this new information as well.

c. Now reverse and let the 1's try it.

d. Things to watch out for:

one shoulder that is higher than the other;

tension in the shoulders or raised shoulders;

habitual leaning on one hip or the other;

one leg shorter than the other (affects hip placement).

Aligned Walking and Sitting

If you're not used to working on your alignment, these exercises may have seemed like hard work. Shake out your body at this time and relax the muscles. Put your hands on your knees and breathe in and out with big, deep breaths.

Now try to recapture once more the perfect aligned position for your body. Feel the ease and strength in this position. Don't you feel tall and in control? Pull in the lower abdominal muscles and feel the power that comes from the center of your body.

From this center, move around the room. Think of the center moving smoothly through space, not of feet plodding from one spot to another. The center of your body describes a smooth line moving parallel to the floor as you move—try to visualize this.

Now take this center over to a chair and control its descent by using your stomach muscles and legs. Come back up out of the chair using the same muscles. Continue your course around the room, moving from the center that you have been exploring.

Here's another one to try in order to control and perceive your body moving through space: Picture your center going from point A to point B. Feel the impetus to move and then move to that point. The sequence is this:

1. get the idea to move;
2. feel, from your center, the impetus to move;
3. move.

Try this several times until you feel comfortable with this process and can recognize it in your own movement patterns.

We do this idea/impetus/move pattern all the time. It helps us as actors to be able to slow the process down and control each step. If we can recognize and control our own movement pattern, we can determine and recreate that of a character.

Review of Neutral Alignment and Moving from the Center

Take time now to review each of these steps toward a neutral body: floor alignment, standing alignment, walking from center, sitting from center, tracing the movement pattern.

By now you have made some exciting discoveries about your own body—you have begun to understand some of the movement patterns that make you an individual. You now can recognize how your body works and what you can do to help it become more comfortable and efficient. Practice the alignment exercises every day until you begin to see a difference in your posture or until others remark how relaxed, good-looking, or assured you are!

A quick note: Society often places a premium on model-like looks. Thank goodness theatre does not have this same mistaken priority. Whatever your body type or shape, there are roles for you. Most directors look for an interesting variety of physical shapes and sizes when casting a show.

This does not mean that you should let yourself get out of shape physically or neglect the postural and centering exercises above. The most versatile and useful actor is one who has discovered his or her neutral body and is capable of clear, strong movement because he or she is in control of that body—not vice versa.

NEUTRAL VOICE

Years ago there was an actress named Judy Holliday. Her voice was high and breathy with a slight New York accent. She was best known for her magnificent portrayal of Billie Dawn, a lady of questionable repute in *Born Yesterday.* Her funny, breathy voice helped to make her a star. But that voice also limited her to roles of the same type for the rest of her career.

I recently worked with an actor whose voice had just gone through its adolescent drop. He had good tone and control when he spoke quietly, but the volume needed at rehearsals destroyed his throat. He loved his role, but he was afraid he would never make it to opening night. This story has a better ending: we worked for two weeks on breathing and tonal exercises. He was fine all through the run of the show.

If you are interested in becoming a versatile actor, you need to discover your own voice—the one that your own body can produce with maximum efficiency and power. You can do this by learning how to **breathe,** how to develop **tone** and **resonance,** and how to pronounce vowels and consonants correctly (**diction** and **articulation**).

EXERCISES

Exercises for Breath

1. Start out on the floor.
    a. Lie down on your back with your knees up, feet flat on the floor, and arms by your side. Lengthen the neck; reach with the top of your head (not the chin).
    Try to feel the floor underneath you with your whole back, even in the curve of the small of your back.
    b. Take a deep breath into the lowest part of your belly. Fill your lungs and let your stomach muscles relax. Now let go of the breath, feeling the stomach muscles and diaphragm returning to their previous position. Repeat this until you are fully aware of the muscular process and have achieved a maximum fullness of breath.

2. Here's another breathing exercise to help you become aware of your breathing potential and develop a greater capacity:
    a. Take a deep breath and pump out four "huh's," making sure that you refill after each one. Once you have mastered this, add a fifth "huh"; sustain it as long as you can. The sequence now is "huh, huh, huh, huh, hu. . . . . . . .h." Have a contest with a classmate to see who can sustain this the longest.

Exercises for Tone and Resonance

In order to achieve maximum tone when you speak, you need to use your resonators (chest, mouth, teeth, bony mask of the face, sinus cavities) instead of forcing the sound out on a heavy stream of breath. A voice that is resonant will carry and last; a voice that is breathy and forced won't do either.

1. Sit forward on your "sitz-bones," tailor fashion, with your back straight. Lengthen your back and neck, straightening the spine.
    a. Focusing on the floor about three feet in front of you, take a deep breath and release it on a breathy "Ah."
    b. Do the same thing again and let the "Ah" float from a high pitch to a low pitch in your own vocal range.
    c. Now try to hold the breath in as you release the "Ah"; feel the resonators in your chest, face, and mouth working to produce tone. Try this a few times, until you can tell the difference in the physical sensation between the breathy "Ah" and the one which is produced by tonal resonators.

2. Roll up to a standing position and try this entire series again. Put your feet about one foot apart and, keeping the spine long, remember to breathe fully before attempting any part of these exercises.

Exercises for Diction and Articulation

Space and time are too limited here to go into much detail about vowels and consonants. A voice and diction course is a necessity for an actor (as is a movement course—or two or five).

1. Vowel purity and consonant cognates:

    There are standard pronunciations for vowels and consonants. Vowels particularly lend themselves to regionalisms and should be worked for a standard American purity. Consonants often come in pairs of voiced and unvoiced.

    Try these sequences:

    P, B, P, B, P, B, P (4 times);
    T, D, T, D, T, D, T, D (4 times);
    K, G, K, G, K, G, K, G (4 times);
    CH, DG, CH, DG, CH, DG, CH, DG (4 times);
    SH, ZH, SH, ZH, SH, ZH, SH, ZH (4 times);
    F, V, F, V, F, V, F, V (4 times);
    TH, TH, TH, TH, TH, TH, TH, TH (4 times).

    Pay attention to how your tongue, lips, teeth, and breath are used to shape the differences in these similar sounds. By making those differences more distinct, your articulation and enunciation will improve.

Exercises for Diction

Development of skills and articulation can best be undertaken in a voice class or comprehensive study program. Search one out. In the meantime, here are three exercises which will help you to develop your articulators. As you say each of these, try for accuracy and clarity. Repeat each of them until you have developed a mastery of the words and can concentrate on the production of clear sound.

1. Tongue twisters.

   Practice each of these tongue twisters until you can say it cleanly and rapidly, giving each vowel and consonant its proper pronunciation.
   a.   Unique New York.
   b.   A bunch of rubber baby buggy bumpers.
   c.   Over the teeth through the tip of the tongue.
   d.   Red leather, yellow leather.

2. Consonant combo: all of the consonant sounds.

   The following exercise contains all of the consonants. Practice it until you are fluent in it.

   Rah, rah; rabababah, racacacah, radadadah, rafafafah, ragagagah, rahahahah, rajajajah, rakakakah, ralalalah, ramamamah, ranananah, rapapapah, raquaquaquah, rarararah, rasasasah, ratatatah, ravavavah, rawawawah, raxaxaxah, rayayayah, razazazah, rachachachacha!

   (Tip: Do in 2/4 rhythm with accent on the first and last syllables. / RA ba ba BAH / RA ca ca CAH like saying "yellow caboose")

3. One-breath poem for consonants and pacing.

   Practice this silly poem until you can say it with good breath control and excellent articulation:
   What' a to-do' to die' today' at a min'ute or two' to two'!
   (A thing' distinct'ly hard' to say', but har'der still' to do'.)
   They'll beat' a tattoo' at twen'ty to two', a rat'atat-tat'atat-too' at two';
   And the dra'gon will come' when he hears' the drum',
   At a min'ute or two' to two' today', at a min'ute or two' to two'!

You can have fun coming up with your own diction exercises. Be sure to warm up your body and voice properly before you leap into articulation exercises, though.

Best of all, get yourself into a voice and diction class and into a movement class and study under teachers who can guide you properly. Do it PRONTO!

Generic Class Syllabi and Schedule

TEXTS REQUIRED

A Beginning Actor's Companion, 3rd Edition, by Lani Harris, Susan Pate, Randy Wonzong, and Donna Breed. (Bring it to class every day.)

ASSIGNMENTS

Performances

1. a short (2 minutes or less) introductory performance or contentless scene. (Not graded)
2. a short 2-person scene (10%)
3. a short 2-person scene or monologue (15%)
4. a final 2-person final scene (25%) (You may do a monologue, if you haven't done one yet.)

Written Work

1. One acting critique, approximately 2–4 pages, typed, double-spaced. (10%)
2. One Character Analysis for a duo scene. Due at performance. (5%)
3. One scored script, with tactics defined for the second scene. Due at performance. (10%)
4. One Character Analysis, plus scored script for final scene. Due the last week of classes. (15%)
5. Class participation or quizzes at the discretion of the instructor. (10%)

SCHEDULE FOR A 15-WEEK SEMESTER

Week

1   Introduction: Course aims, philosophy of acting; acting exercises.
    Read Chapter One.

2   Basics of acting: intention, obstacle: performance exercises.
    Read Chapter Two.

3   Analysis for performance: analysis techniques, character analysis; demonstration activities; performance exercises. Read Chapter Three.

4   Acting skills: relationship, emotions, stakes, beats; technique exercises.

5   1st Scene Performance Previews.

6   1st Scene Performance: 1st paper due: character analysis.
        Read Chapter Four.

7   Making actor choices: tactics; demonstration activities.
        Read Chapters Five and Six.

8   Critiquing acting: description, evaluation, evidence; rehearsal and ethics.
        Read Chapter Seven.

9   A character's inner life: discoveries, realizations, subtext, in the moment; demonstration activities; critique paper due. Read Chapter Eight.

10   2nd Duet Performance Previews.

11   2nd Duet Performances. Read Chapter Nine.

12   Scoring: mapping tactics, discoveries, and realizations; Read Chapter 10.

13   More actor tools: body, voice, and movement; technique activities.
        Read Chapter 11.

14   Final Duet Performance Previews.

15   Final Duet Performances; 2nd analysis paper due: scoring the action.

Glossary

Acting

Putting yourself on the line, expressing what you have inside you, delving into what is inside others, observing life so that you can portray it by performing dramatic material, either alone or with others. A character in a given circumstance that uses tactics to overcome obstacles which prevent the achievement of an intention.

Advocacy of Character

Getting inside your character's skin so you can understand why the character does what he does; behaving as your character and fighting as hard as he does to achieve the character's intentions. Believing in what your character wants, and creating strong justifications, even if your character is a "villain."

As If

An acting tool which allows the actor to transfer personal experience to the performance of the character; finding parallels between your experiences and the character's life.

Biographical Analysis

The process of determining all the pertinent information about the character's life, background, situation, and circumstance.

Blocking

The movement of the actors about the stage; also the process of working out this movement and patterns of movement.

Collaboration

Working together to create something which you could not have created as an individual; the process of developing and sharing the process of artistic discovery with an acting partner.

Commitment to Character

Performing a character to your fullest capacity. Using all of your mental, physical, and emotional energy to bring the character to life; the very opposite of just learning your lines and saying them out loud.

Conflict

The clash between opposing characters; the results when a character runs into and attempts to deal with obstacles that stand in the way of achieving an intention.

Contentless Scene

A scene in which the words, by themselves, do not clearly reveal any specific characters or story. It is a scene that has no specified dramatic content until the actors make up and add these specific elements themselves.

Creative Listening

Thinking as the character and listening for clues from the other characters about how you are doing and how you need to change or modify your tactics to succeed in your intention.

Creative Responsiveness

Being open and willing to change your responses and choices on stage as your character is changing and adjusting; the inventive process of making your acting more alive.

Critiquing

Looking at a performance to recognize and discuss choices the actor made. The process can be objective—descriptive criticism—or it can be judgmental—evaluative criticism. In the latter you contrast what the actor did with what might have or should have been done.

Descriptive Criticism

The process of talking about the observable, factual parts of a performance; it tells what the audience saw in a performance, not what should, ought, or might have been done. It is reporting, not judgmental.

Discoveries

New external information. Those points in a scene or play where the character (usually suddenly) becomes aware of physical information from the outside world which has some bearing on achieving an intention.

Evaluative Criticism

The process of describing a performance in terms of what did and did not work; judging the performance according to what it was and what it could or should have been. It is the process of making value judgments.

Given Circumstances

The available information in the play itself which tells us about the time, place, action, details, and all the available background of the characters and the situation they are in.

Intention

The thing the character wants to achieve right now; the immediate goal—the aim—that will lead to the desired outcome the character hopes to achieve. (see also *Nested Intentions.*)

Intentional Acting

The process of playing a character by acting out the intentions of what the character hopes to achieve; it is the opposite of emotional acting—playing emotions instead of character—which is a very weak approach.

Moments

Those points in the action of a scene or play when the character gains new insight, figures something out; those points—like in cartoons—where the light bulb goes on over the character's head. They include realizations, discoveries, and tactic changes.

Muscle Memory

The process of training the body (both its emotional and physical components) to perform repetitious functions automatically, or at least without having to give much conscious thought to their enactment.

Nested Intentions

The various goals a character hopes to achieve in the various scenes of the play; in addition to some overall intention for the whole play, the character has numerous short-term goals as well—all are stacked inside the overall goal or intention the character has throughout the play.

Neutral Body

A body free of specific character traits—a body which allows you to make and show your audience clear physical choices about what your character's body is like and how your character uses it.

Neutral Voice

A voice free of specific character traits—it is without mannerism, full of rich tone, and uses Standard American Stage Speech.

Obstacle

What keeps a character from achieving an intention; the thing (person, object, idea, fear, concern, etc.) which stands in the way.

Objective or Super-Objective

Your character's ultimate goal for the play. (Intentions are the smaller, moment-to-moment goals that will ultimately lead to achieving the larger objective or super-objective for the play.)

Realization

New internal information. Those points in a scene or play where the character (usually suddenly) becomes aware of information from inside him- or herself which has some bearing on achieving an intention.

Rehearsal Journal

A systematic process which helps you to plan out and keep track of your rehearsals. A step-by-step means of developing your character through working with the text and your partner.

Rehearse

The process of going over a scene, either alone or with your partner, to come up with, try out, and perfect choices of action which will make your character more clear and more complete for your audience during performance.

Scene Analysis

Breaking a scene down into its various elements, the better to understand how the scene itself works and how your character responds to the ongoing action of the scene as it unfolds.

Scoring *(practice on scene for "A coupla white chicks ..."*

The process of breaking down a scene, speech, or monologue into its separate action steps; it maps out and makes specific the sequence of choices the character makes in playing out the scene.

Stage Fright

The normal reaction most humans feel when faced with the prospect of being in front of an audience; a phenomenon easily controlled with a few simple exercises and modest training.

Stakes

The extent or degree to which the character wants to achieve an intention; the higher the stakes the more badly, more desperately, more completely the character wants this.

Tactics

The specific actions a character takes to overcome the obstacles standing in the way of desired intentions. The moment-to-moment involvement of the character, who is constantly selecting and acting out these actions. The choice of tactics forms a strategy to achieve the objective.

Truthful Feelings

If you commit to your character's inner life honestly in performance, the audience will respond; they will empathize with you because you will have touched their emotions and reminded them of their own experiences.